How to Think Like Sir Alex Ferguson

'A fascinating insight into the mind and methods of the most successful coach in British history. Sir Alex Ferguson, as Damian Hughes so adeptly reveals, was not just a football manager. He was a lot more than that. Psychologist, motivator, mentor and disciplinarian, he perfected all of the attributes needed to be a successful manager in any business. And invented a few of his own.'

Jim White, *Telegraph*

'Elite coaching and leadership is about making the comfortable uncomfortable whilst helping the uncomfortable to become comfortable with change. Sir Alex Ferguson was the very best at that and Professor Damian Hughes has produced a compelling book which explains how he did this. I couldn't put it down and I am confident that you will find much in here to help you achieve success in your own chosen field.'

Charles van Commenee,
UK Athletics and 2012 GB Olympic Head Coach

'Damian Hughes challenges traditional coaching methods by encouraging coaches to maintain strong principles supported by self-awareness and the ability to adapt and change through the myriad of leadership challenges (and opportunities!). In this excellent book, Damian's inquisitive and insightful mind breaks down one of the greatest coaches in the history of sport. With examples from Sir Alex Ferguson's distinguished career, he masterfully illustrates a range of key principles which can be applied by any fan, coach or business leader.'

Trent Robinson,
Head coach Sydney Roosters Rugby League,
Coach of the Year, 2014

How to Think Like Sir Alex Ferguson

The Business of Winning and Managing Success

By Professor Damian Hughes

Aurum
Press

First published in Great Britain
2014 by Aurum Press Ltd
74–77 White Lion Street
Islington
London N1 9PF
www.aurumpress.co.uk

A catalogue record for this book is available from the British
Library.

ISBN 978 1 78131 348 0

5 7 9 10 8 6
2016 2018 2017 2015

Typeset in Perpetua by Saxon Graphics Ltd, Derby
Printed by CPI Group (UK) Ltd, Croydon, CR0 4YY

Contents

Preface

What does successful change look like?

Many of us grow up instinctively believing that successful change can best be described as a direct trajectory where sufficiently determined performance leads to the inevitable desired outcome.

It's a myth.

Harvard professor Rosabeth Moss Kanter highlights how everyone loves and remembers inspiring beginnings and happy endings. It is the part in between we often fail to appreciate, where the hard work kicks in and the tough challenges emerge. At these moments, we experience Kanter's Law: 'Everything can look like a failure in the middle'. Sir Alex Ferguson understood this law, not least because he spent a large part of his Manchester United career successfully battling his way through it. He preferred to explain this philosophy with the more prosaic: 'Success doesn't happen in straight lines.'

Ferguson had taken over at United when the club was at perhaps its lowest point since the tragedy of the Munich air disaster. It had experienced a startling fall from grace since the European Cup triumph of 1968, and had not won an English League title in nearly twenty years. By prioritising the development of young players, rebuilding the team, being shrewd in the transfer market, emphasising attacking football and bringing the best out of his players, Ferguson eventually turned United's fortunes around. He delivered football of rare beauty. He bought Eric Cantona, the rebel with a cause. He nurtured the Golden Generation. He discovered Ole Gunnar Solskjaer, the baby-faced assassin. He signed Wayne Rooney, the assassin-faced baby. He brought trophies, glory, prestige and the kind of happiness, over twenty-six years, that United supporters had once only dreamed of. No one has managed at the highest level for so long. Or with such competitive courage. Nobody has beaten the system the way he has and accumulated so many trophies.

Two decades on, Old Trafford is a gleaming all-seater stadium. Its capacity has risen from 56,000 to 76,000 and the 'Keep Off The Grass' signs are in five different languages. It has been an epic journey of 6 a.m. starts, nerve-shredding football and relentless drama. Before his retirement in May 2013, Ferguson outlasted thirteen different Manchester City managers.

He saw off Prime Ministers Thatcher, Major, Blair and Brown. He was knighted and immortalised in bronze, and he turned United into one of the most prolific trophy-grabbing machines in the modern game. Thirteen League titles, two European Cups, five FA Cups, one European Cup Winners' Cup, two League Cups, plus enough individual awards to fill a museum – it amounts to an overall haul nearly double that of the next most successful English club manager.

Yet he did not have it all his own way. Over the years he had to learn to manage his own very human fears and insecurities whilst attempting to convince a demanding and sceptical public and media that he knew what he was doing. He also had to respond to several major challengers: besides seeing United replace close rival Liverpool FC as the club holding the most English League titles, he successfully battled the fluid style of play which had brought London-based Arsenal FC three titles in the late 1990s and early 2000s, triumphed over the hundreds of millions of dollars Russian billionaire owner Roman Abramovich had invested in Chelsea FC, and in his final season took the championship from Manchester City, the home town rivals he once famously referred to as United's 'noisy neighbours', who had switched owners and invested unprecedented amounts of money in new players.

Sir Alex Ferguson was a manager of uncommon ability.

Yet Ferguson was far more than a manager. He played a central role in the whole Manchester United organisation, managing not just the first team but the entire club, casting it in his own image. If all institutions take their lead from the head – for example, Virgin is perceived as the gutsy underdog; slightly dippy, eccentric, a corporation with a beard and sweater, like Sir Richard Branson, its boss – then at Ferguson's Manchester United, everyone had to embrace change. 'Steve Jobs was Apple; Sir Alex Ferguson is Manchester United,' said the club's former chief executive David Gill and if there was one quality that defined his success, it was 'the tremendous capacity to adapt and keep performing as the game has changed'. In his own reflections on how he achieved such unprecedented success, Ferguson maintained that, 'The thing I've done well over the years is manage change. You control change by accepting it. Most people don't look to change. But I always felt I couldn't afford *not* to change.'

Sir Alex Ferguson now shares with the business students of Harvard University the insights he learned in the exacting crucible of his 26-year tenure as Manchester United manager. This book now offers you too, many of those ideas on how to make change happen.

The Purpose of this Book

In this book, I want to explore two ideas.

First I want to capture how Sir Alex Ferguson did as he said and embraced change in order to remain at the forefront of one of the world's most competitive industries, where the failure rate is high (the average tenure of a manager in football is just one year and four months) and forgiveness for mistakes is so low (55 per cent of first-time managers never work again). I want to dig deeper than the popular caricature of a flint-faced authority figure, ranting at the match officials and pointing to his stopwatch. For that is exactly what it is: a caricature.

The real Ferguson is far more complex than the tabloid portrayal. He isn't always 'fuming' or 'exploding'. He doesn't always 'slam' and 'blast'. On his worst days, his enemies would describe him as dictatorial, hostile and standoffish. But even they would concede that he can also be warm, charming and convivial, with kind edges and an infectious laugh.

Ferguson is a natural storyteller. He has an outstanding memory for the smallest pieces of information, and varied interests beyond the four white lines that have contained much of his life. He has taught himself French using audiocassettes. He has learned to play the piano. He 'gets' jazz. He has a global knowledge when it comes to food and is a connoisseur of fine wines. He is a man of fierce intellect and a student of human nature with an impressively high IQ and an astute appreciation of what makes other people tick. It is this final attribute, his deep understanding of human nature and the techniques he employed as a manager to extract the finest qualities from it, that we will also explore.

This book will appeal to many people from different camps. At one level, it is written for anyone in any field of endeavour – business, education, government, non-profit, the arts – and any context where individuals lead other individuals and teams in their pursuit of success in changing times. At another level, it is written unashamedly for football fans: the men and women who love the game, and who – like me – are simply fascinated by insights from the career of a man who reigned at the apex of his profession for over thirty years. We want to know how and why Sir Alex Ferguson managed to do what he did.

This is not to say that one manager has all the answers. But there is a set of circumstances from which emerges a compelling language of leading change that will be useful to leaders in any and every setting and culture.

The second purpose of this book is to show how these same techniques and approaches can be adopted and used by you, the reader, and related to successfully meeting your own challenges. By using examples from Ferguson's Manchester United career, along with a wide range of other non-footballing examples and illustrations, I intend to help you identify within these pages some of your own struggles, challenges and successes and to create a language from these that will enhance your own practices.

The playwright Alan Bennett once suggested that there should be a notice hanging in the entrance to the National Gallery saying:

You don't have to like everything here

Alex Ferguson admiringly said something similar about Ryan Giggs's capacity to cope with the hype that surrounded him and discern what is useful from what is not: 'He's got a bullshit detector in his head.'

It is a thought worth adopting for this book too. If we strive too hard looking for a perfect answer, we can be dismissive and absolute in our judgements of anything less. There is no obligation for you to agree with or do everything suggested in this book. Whilst I want you to walk away having finished the book and be able to apply the ideas directly to your own life for immediate effect, it is not set out as a step-by-step guide. I want to give you more than just a set of prescriptions. As Ferguson discovered, some of the ideas suggested will not work all of the time, but all of them will work some of the time. Above all, the book is designed to give you insights, ideas and support about managing change in your life.

Think of this book in your hands as being like your own version of Sir Alex Ferguson, prompting, questioning and helping you deal with change. Read the lessons, do the exercises that are appropriate and answer the questions posed if they are relevant to your circumstances. If you do, you will acquire the skills needed to see change as something positive.

Character for Change

Attitude is a little thing that makes a big difference.
Winston Churchill

'I was standing in the canteen queue for my lunch,' says Robbie Brady, the young Irish footballer who played at Manchester United for six years from the age of sixteen. Cristiano Ronaldo, the Portuguese player since described by Sir Alex Ferguson as 'the best footballer I've ever managed', had emerged from the shower and sauntered towards the same queue.

'I thought I was being polite,' Brady recalls, 'and invited him to join the queue in front of me and thought no more of it.'

As he left the canteen, he was surprised to be beckoned over by the clearly agitated manager.

'Why did you do that?' Ferguson asked.

'What?' asked the nonplussed Brady.

'Allow Cristiano into the queue ahead of you?'

'I tried to explain that I thought I was being polite,' laughs Brady, adding what he thought was an obvious caveat: 'and it is Ronaldo, the best player in the world.'

Ferguson stopped him in his tracks. 'I want you to think you're better than him. I want you to believe you can take his place in the team. I don't want you to be subservient to him. Don't do it again,' he warned.

This small, seemingly insignificant tale contains an illustration of one of Ferguson's prime assets, a deep understanding of human nature, of 'character', as he calls it. He was constantly looking for those who, like him, possessed the unreasonableness, the stubbornness, the willingness to embrace challenges and meet change head-on.

There is a story that Walt Disney employed similar levels of analysis when he was recruiting executives to work alongside him. At meal times, he would watch whether a candidate put salt onto their food before tasting it. He viewed this action as a sign of inflexible thinking; after all, if a person was not prepared to at least taste a meal before adding their own changes, this behaviour would transfer to the workplace.

When describing the characteristics he was searching for in a player, Ferguson said, 'To meet the challenge of staying at United and being the best, you need to have the right character. The character to show courage to want the ball under pressure and the urge to take risks with it. Anyone can demand the ball when we are winning comfortably, courage is to want it when we are getting beat and under pressure.' Many of us are bad at judging this trait because we instinctively tend to overrate the obvious, more visible actions, and underrate the less glamorous traits. Which, if we employ Ferguson's phrase and call them 'character' – namely work habits, competitiveness, ambition and grit – turn out to be far more important in the long run.

Ole Gunnar Solskjaer, the Norwegian striker who played for Ferguson before coaching alongside him, described how Ferguson had taught him to avoid this trap when selecting players to work with. He explained how the young striker Danny Welbeck had impressed as an apprentice because of his willingness to stay behind and help collect stray footballs after the practice had ended. 'He showed he was a real team player,' was the conclusion. In short, Ferguson figured out an efficient way to test for character. Here's how it worked: he would invite the prospect to a meeting. The player walked in, Ferguson said a brisk hello, clicked off the lights, then pressed the PLAY button to start a video of one of the player's worst moments. Then he would turn to the player and ask, 'So what happened there?'

At such a moment Ferguson was not really interested in what happened, of course. He was interested in how the player reacted to adversity. How did their brain handle failure? Did they take responsibility, or make excuses? Did they blame others, or talk about what they would do differently? The idea was not just to weed out people with the wrong mindset, but also to identify those who had the right one. 'There are lots of young men who like the idea of being a footballer but don't want to invest the time to work at being a footballer,' is how he explained it.

In March 1993, Ferguson applied this principle with a cohort of young players who were beginning to show rare talent. David Beckham, Ryan Giggs, Gary Neville and Paul Scholes were required to analyse their best and worst performances both in writing and then in mock television interviews. Long-serving Manchester broad-casters Jimmy Wagg and Eamonn O'Neal ran the training whilst Ferguson and Paul McGuinness, the head of the highly successful youth set-up, looked on.

The results make fascinating reading, not least for the unsparing nature of the players' self-assessment. 'I played crap. I didn't do too well, really. Just nothin' was going right. Nothin' went our way,' wrote a surprisingly frank David Beckham in his assessment of his own worst performance. When he was interviewed, his shy smile could not disguise the steeliness of his ambition. By working hard, he said, 'I hope to play for United's first team in the next couple of years and emulate my hero, Bryan Robson.'

In his notes, Giggs couldn't think of a single match he'd played well in and chose to leave a blank space. He did, however, note that one performance against Oldham wasn't good enough, writing: 'I got marked out of the game and I must of kicked the ball about twice.' Gary Neville, now famous for his incisive analysis as a television pundit, analysed his poorest performance, the 1993 Youth Cup final second leg against Leeds, in a blunt, forthright fashion: 'My arsehole dropped out. Didn't feel in the game.'

'It was obvious, even then, that these guys would go on to enjoy impressive careers,' O'Neal recalls. 'They didn't make excuses for their failures and they didn't dwell on their successes. Ferguson sat smiling throughout.'

Ferguson employed a similar approach with all of the 212 players he chose to join his cause. 'I liked to refer to it as the working-class principle,' he explains. 'Not all players come from a working-class background, but maybe their fathers do, or their grandfathers, and I found it useful to remind players how far they have come. I would tell them that having a work ethic is very important. It seemed to enhance their pride. I would remind them that it is trust in one another, not letting their mates down, that helps build their character.'

In psychology, what he was doing was using a concept called the self-consistency theory. This means that we act according to the image we hold of ourselves. Prescott Lecky, one of the pioneers of this self-image psychology, believes that humans have an inherent need for consistency. If a thought is inconsistent with other stronger ideas and concepts, the mind will reject it. One example of how this works is illustrated by the mental illness anorexia. If a sufferer regards themselves as being overweight, despite the obvious evidence to the contrary in a mirror, they will only see an over-weight reflection staring back, prompting them to continue their destructive weight-loss behaviour. The self-consistency theory means that we act according to the image we hold of ourselves. When we assign a behaviour or characteristic to a person (or even to ourselves), then make a request that is consistent with that behaviour, that person will naturally strive to demonstrate it. This is why Ferguson's response to young Robbie Brady's behaviour and his continued emphasis on the importance of character were so perceptive.

Lecky recounts a story about one of his patients, a salesman who was afraid to call on top management clients. Lecky asked him, 'Would you get down on all fours and crawl into the office, prostrating yourself before a superior personage?'

'I should say not!' the salesman replied.

'Then why do you mentally crawl and cringe? Can't you see that you are doing essentially the same thing when you go in overly concerned with whether or not they will approve of you? Can't you see you are literally begging for their approval of you as a person?'

When Robbie Brady let Cristiano Ronaldo jump in front of him at the queue, Ferguson interpreted it as the behaviour of someone who did not believe he was equal to the Portuguese player. If he did not believe it, the influence of the best coaching in the world would not have any effect.

What is your character like when facing change?

So how would you fare in a test of your character's capacity to embrace change?

If I asked you to come up with words to describe change, what would you say? Many people suggest a mixture of negative and positive terms. On the one hand, *fear*, *anxiety*, *loss*, *danger* and *panic*; on the other, *exhilaration*, *risk-taking*, *excitement*, *improvements*, *energising*. Which words do you most associate with the prospect?

In GE Global Research's findings about change programmes in business, it was established that 100 per cent of changes rated as 'successful' had a good technical solution or approach. The same research also highlighted that over 98 per cent of changes rated as 'unsuccessful' also had a good technical solution or approach. The critical difference between the successful and unsuccessful changes was not the approach. It was the people involved – and how they responded to change. When another legendary football manager, Brian Clough – a man who never lacked confidence in his own character – was asked by the press what made him believe that he was best suited to the job of changing the fortunes of Nottingham Forest, his face remained completely deadpan, he looked at the reporters and offered the classic footballing mathematical observation that 'Ninety per cent of the game is half mental.'

When facing times of change, how important do you think character is?

Maybe I can lead you to an answer.

Let's begin with a simple exercise. It will help you discover what Ferguson meant when assessing his ability to manage change – that once you reach a certain level of competence, it's your character that becomes most important.

Sit back and recall a time when you were performing at your very best. Picture a time when you were at the top of your game, when every move and decision you made was the right one, when it seemed like everything went your way. Dr Jim Loehr, one of the world's leading sports psychologists, describes this state as 'when we are physically relaxed, mentally calm, fearless, energised, positively happy, effortless, automatic and confident.' Imagine that you are watching a film of your highlights on TV. You feel exactly as Dr Loehr describes and have no fear, no anxieties and no self-doubt. Everything is flowing and going your way. Look around. Where are you? What time of day is it? What are you wearing? Who is with you? Who is watching? What do you hear? Breathe in the air. What do you smell? Visualise that pleasurable experience in plenty of detail, then take a piece of paper and try to capture your thoughts on it.

Next, let that image slowly fade, and in its place recall your worst ever day. Think of the event or experience when you felt weakest and most ineffective, when nothing went your way, no matter how hard you tried. Again, write down how this felt.

Now leave that memory behind and fast-forward back into the present. With Brian Clough's quote in mind, compare yourself when operating at your very best and at your very worst. Then honestly answer this question:

What percentage of the difference was mental?

When I do this exercise with leaders, I get everyone in the room to stand up. I ask those who think the mental part was less than 10 per cent of the difference to sit down. Those who think that it was less than 20 per cent are then asked to take a seat. I repeat this process for those who believe that it is less than 30 per cent and then 40 per cent. When I finally get to 50 per cent at least half the room remains standing. What about you? Would you still be on your feet?

If the answer to this question is yes, then answer my next question: if you believe that the difference between your very best and your worst day when leading change was, as Clough said, at least 50 per cent mental, then how much time do you actually spend on understanding the psychology of change and how it can help you cope under the pressures it brings?

That's where this book comes in.

See Change

You cannot hit what you cannot see.

Muhammad Ali

Date: Wednesday, 26 May 1999
Time: 9.45 p.m. EST
Location: Camp Nou Football Stadium, Barcelona

The early summer sun descended below the horizon yet the humidity ensured that the temperature remained warm. As Pierluigi Collina, the tall, distinctive Italian referee, blew a shrill whistle to signal the end of the first forty-five minutes, fifty-five thousand Manchester United fans, the largest ever mass of people to leave the UK since D-Day, and subsequently described by the Catalan daily newspaper *La Vanguardia* as 'ugly but good people', greeted its blast with a collective sigh of disappointment.

After the power and energy which had defined their season, capturing the League and FA Cup double along the way, this was the Reds' most muted showing, and it had happened on the biggest stage of all, the UEFA Champions League final. Their German rivals, Bayern Munich, had taken the lead early and had never looked in danger of relinquishing this advantage in the following thirty-nine minutes.

'Poor,' opined Ron Atkinson, the football manager who had preceded Alex Ferguson as United boss, and was now commentating on the game. 'This is the challenge of a lifetime for Ferguson. He has to come up with something special now.' Imagine that you are wearing Ferguson's shoes as you make the steep descent into the bowels of the Camp Nou and stride towards the dressing room, knowing that you have approximately eight minutes to draw upon all of your motivational skills to rouse the team from an un-inspired, un-United display. This is the closest you have been to your last great ambition, winning the trophy you have long coveted and which represents the opportunity to be bracketed alongside your own heroes, Jock Stein and Matt Busby, as a managerial great. ('Europe has become my personal crusade. I must win the European Cup to be considered as a great manager,' are the words you remember saying to the press.) The pressure mounting upon your shoulders seems to increase with every step. You catch the furtive glances in your direction from the coaching staff. You hear the disquiet from your players as they crash into the dressing room, expressing their bitter disappointment. Above all, you sense the hope – the trust – that you can deliver a good half-time team talk. A *great* half-time team talk.

You think through the options that you could employ:

1. You could deliver an instinctive, creative, last-minute, improvised burst of genius that will change everything. A fight-them-on-the-beaches epic to arouse, a Gettysburg address to inspire, an oration so dizzying, so game-changing it might have transformed Churchill himself into a vibrant centre forward, made Abraham Lincoln a useful box-to-box man.
2. You could lose your temper and tell them in rich, colourful terms how disappointed you are.
3. You could employ cognitive dissonance.

Which one will you choose?

1. You know those creative, last-minute, improvised bursts of genius that change everything: the revolutionary strategy, the brilliant eleventh-hour gambit, the heart-lifting pre-game speech? Think Al Pacino in *Any Given Sunday*, Samuel L. Jackson

in *Coach Carter*. This is a myth born in Hollywood where the coach is portrayed as a genius. It doesn't happen.

2. You lost your temper once before in this very stadium when you shouted at Paul Ince for continually giving away possession. ('You fucking bottler. You've lost me the European Cup, Ince. Are you happy?') The approach didn't work then; you were defeated 4–0 by Barcelona.

3. You remain measured, calm and to the point and remember something Steve Archibald, a player you managed at Aberdeen, had told you about the awful emptiness of losing a European Cup with Barcelona.

'If you lose, you'll go up to collect losers' medals and you'll be six feet away from the European Cup,' Ferguson said as the players prepared themselves for the second half. 'But you won't be able to touch it. I want you to think about the fact you'll have been so close to it and for many of you that will be the closest you'll ever get. And you will hate the thought for the rest of your lives. So just make sure you don't come back in here without giving your all.' The number of those players who have subsequently recounted the effect of his words, and cited their influence in what was to come, suggests the message certainly hit the mark.

Striker Andy Cole, who was sitting opposite Ferguson as he delivered his talk, says, 'I thought about what a great feeling it would be to actually lift that trophy, to know that you've achieved something you've wanted to do since being a kid.' Dutch defender Jaap Stam says, 'The speech ignited a go-get-'em attitude which spread through the team.' Cole's strike partner Dwight Yorke agrees. 'That tale did more to inspire the players than a hairdryer, or a kung-fu kick.' Meanwhile, quietly warming up in the background, Ole Gunnar Solskjaer was also employing the same psychological theory, pioneered by Leon Festinger, a leading research psychologist, who explained that the conscious mind can hold two opposing ideas at the same time. Such conflict (or dissonance) between these ideas creates a psychological tension which throws our system out of order. When this happens, there is a part of our subconscious, known as the creative subconscious, which springs into action. Among its key functions is maintaining order in our lives. When our system is thrown out of order by an alternative vision of how things could or should be, we get a surge of energy to resolve the tension and put things back in order, the way they should be or instead, move to the new state. Gestalt psychologists clumsily call this the 'out-of-order-into-order-process'.

'I was attempting to catch Ferguson's eye,' Solskjaer recalls. 'The manager had a little chat with Teddy

Sheringham, to say that he was going to put him on. I was just in the background, hoping he comes over to me, but he didn't.

'All the while, I was thinking: "Why don't you put me on?" I had recently come on as a substitute and scored important goals against Liverpool and Nottingham Forest. I had a premonition I was going to do something that night. I could see myself scoring the winning goal.' In fact, he had phoned his best friend in Norway and told him, 'Something big is going to happen for me tonight.'

With eighty-five minutes gone and Manchester United still behind, those who had not been privy to Ferguson's speech assumed it was all over. United legend George Best had left the stadium looking for a bar, unwilling to watch his team lose. Lennart Johansson, the UEFA president, had headed down to pitchside to prepare to present the trophy to Bayern Munich. In the press box, most of the assembled English journalists were busy filing the first takes of reports to the effect that Ferguson had failed. Much of that copy would survive in the next day's first editions. Ferguson would keep those copies in his office for posterity.

By the time Johansson came out of the tunnel to take up his position, the score was 1–1. Teddy Sheringham, on as a substitute, scrambled the ball home from close in. With extra time now looking inevitable, Johansson turned to make his way back upstairs. On the bench, the United staff began urging the manager to rearrange the team, to get them back into shape for the additional thirty minutes. But Ferguson wasn't listening: 'The Bayern players had lost all positional discipline: they were like men staggering away from a plane crash,' he says. 'I knew that they'd gone, mentally.' The cup was six feet away from him but now within reach. 'This game isn't finished yet,' he said on the touchline to Steve McClaren, his assistant.

He was watching the ball spin off a Bayern player for another corner. 'Can United score? They always score,' suggested Clive Tyldesley, the match commentator. Beckham took the corner kick. Sheringham flicked it on. And Solskjaer, who had been on the field for just ten minutes and had noticed opposing defender Samuel Kuffour's tendency to close his eyes when he headed the ball, reacted ahead of his dumbfounded, and soon to be traumatised, Bayern marker to stick out his right leg, prod the ball into the roof of the net and win the game. In the immediate aftermath, Ferguson rejected the opportunity to explain to the equally shell-shocked viewing public how the 'out-of-order-into-order-process' was complete, choosing instead to reflect, 'Football. Bloody hell!'

When Kelvin MacKenzie, the former editor of the *Sun* newspaper, decided to sack the paper's astrologer, he began his letter of dismissal with the words, 'As you may already have foreseen …' Many people have a similarly cynical view when it is suggested that we have the ability to see into the future. However, you would never think of jumping into a taxi and, when the driver asks you, 'Where to?' replying, 'I don't know, just take me anywhere.' The chances are you will have a clear idea where you want to go. You see, you can visualise the future, but most of us don't actively do it to help us deal with change.

When I interview leaders, my favourite interview question is: 'Where do you see yourself in two years' time?'

Most interviewees stutter and stumble over their answers, as they don't really have a clue. How about you? Would you be able to offer a clear response? In my experience, about 10 per cent of people respond confidently as they have a clear view about their own future. However, 90 per cent of us tend to stay stuck in the immediate present or in the past. Whenever someone responds to my question by saying, 'Never mind two years from now, I don't even know where I'll be two minutes from now,' it's true. They can't think about the future because they don't believe, deep down, that they have any real influence over it.

This belief is even more profound during times of change. Most of us accept, without any question, that we are the victims of – rather than the creators of –

change. Ferguson's answer to this same question, posed by the boffins of Harvard University, was unequivocally clear. 'The cycle of a successful team lasts maybe four years and then some change is needed. I tried to visualise the team three or four years ahead and make decisions accordingly,' he said. 'The goal is to evolve gradually and so it is mainly about two things. First: who did we have coming through and where did we see them in three years' time; and second, [what] were the signs that existing players were getting older.' His use of visualisation and his willingness to project forward helped him make tough decisions. 'The hardest part is to let go of a player who has been a great guy. If you see the change, the deterioration, you have to ask yourself what things are going to be like two years ahead.'

One example of this was his observation of his talismanic playmaker Eric Cantona. When Cantona arrived at the club in 1992, Ferguson marvelled at his attitude. 'Manchester United can be a daunting place for some people and it has destroyed one or two of them over the years. But Eric Cantona just swaggered in, stuck out his chest and looked around. He surveyed everything as though he were asking: I'm Cantona, how big are you? Are you big enough for me? I knew we had something special then.'

However, in early 1997, Ferguson began to notice a subtle change. 'There was a dullness in his eyes,' he observed in the months before Cantona came to recognise it himself. 'I had to acknowledge that perhaps he was right to terminate his career before blatant decline became an insult to the fierce pride that burned in him.' Cantona retired in the summer.

'He's never really looking at this moment, he's always looking into the future,' Ryan Giggs marvelled of Ferguson. 'Knowing what needs strengthening and what needs refreshing – he's got that knack.' This perspective is exactly what separates those who thrive in times of change. They know that everything is created twice. They understand that you must clearly see future success in your mind's eye before you can begin to create it in reality. They vividly imagine what successful change means to them until it becomes so familiar that as far as their unconscious mind is concerned, they have already achieved it. When they do this, the brain and the body can't tell the difference between something which is vividly imagined and reality.

Let's briefly discuss the science bit to understand how this happens and how it can help you to deal with change.

Dendrites

Thomas Edison suggested that his success 'owed more to his imagination than facts'. Edison, one of the most prolific inventors of all time, used to tackle the problems caused by change by making time for himself to sit on a tin tray with a stone between his knees. As he started to think about how he'd deal with his problems, he would relax and access his subconscious mind. When he daydreamed too deeply, he would fall asleep and lose consciousness, causing the stone to drop on to the tin and wake him up. He would then begin the process all over again and ensure that he had maximum time to think and visualise himself solving problems. United and England striker Wayne Rooney has honed a similar technique to help him master the challenges posed on the football field. 'When a cross comes into the box, there's so many things that go through your mind in a split second, like five or six different things you can do with the ball,' he says.

'Part of my preparation is I go and ask the kit man what colour we're wearing – if it's red top, white shorts, white socks or black socks. Then I lie in bed the night before the game and visualise myself scoring goals or doing well. You're trying to put yourself in that moment and trying to prepare yourself, to have a "memory" before the game. I don't know if you'd call it visualising or dreaming, but I've always done it, my whole life.'

This is because whenever we create a thought or perform an action, like throwing a ball, our brain's cells, or neurons to give them their proper name, connect with each other. Once those neurons come together, they stay linked forever by the chemical reaction that occurs. These links between our brain cells are called dendrites.

Once you form a dendrite, every time you repeat the same action or thought the chemical link gets thicker and the dendrite gets wider. The more you repeat the same thought or action, the wider it gets. Think of it like going from a narrow lane, to a road, to a dual carriageway and eventually to a motorway, allowing the chemical to travel at an ever greater pace. Eventually, this means that your reactions improve; you do things more quickly and almost without any conscious effort.

Here's an example you can try in the office.

Find a ball and throw it to someone and then ask them to throw it back to you. Do it again, a little faster this time. Do this a few times, throwing the ball back and forth until you are both doing it comfortably and easily. Now, go to throw the ball, but hold on to it instead, just making your partner think you are going to throw it. What happens? The chances are they will move their hands and try to catch it, even though you have kept hold of it. Remember, our brain doesn't know the difference between a real and an imagined experience, and so the brain would have reacted to a ball being thrown because the dendrite which has been built to react to that action is now bigger than the one which lets us stay still. This is the same reason why Wayne Rooney, like Ole Gunnar Solskjaer before him, is able to react before his opponents move, and Alex Ferguson was able to spot a decline in a player before the player knew it himself.

There is another way to prove how powerful your thoughts are. This particular exercise was first demonstrated by a nineteenth-century French doctor, Hippolyte Bernheim, who also taught Sigmund Freud, and spent many years investigating the connection between the mind and body. He called it the 'ideomotor response' (from idea + movement), and the chances are you have already experienced the same effect if you have ever found yourself involuntarily kicking an imaginary ball whilst watching a game of football or making sudden brief empathetic movements when watching a film.

First, make yourself a pendulum. You'll need to attach a small weight (a couple of keys will work, or a heavy finger ring is ideal) to about eight inches of string. Sit or stand comfortably and hold the top of the string so that the weight just hangs down. Let it rest motionless and make sure that your hand, elbow and arm are able to move freely. Now close your eyes and focus on the weight. Imagine that it is able to swing back and forth. Create a picture of this, swinging slowly at first then starting to pick up speed. If it helps, you can either imagine something pulling it, or a force surrounding it – whatever helps to fire your imagination. But keep your hand completely still. Do this in your mind for about a minute, and then open your eyes. Your pendulum will now be swinging from side to side. It doesn't matter how large the swing, although the larger the swing the bigger and more vivid your mental picture is. The reason for this is that your mind *wanted* to respond. The effect is caused by the involuntary muscle movements of the hand, triggered by your own mental pictures. This means that a thought or idea will cause tiny micro-muscular movements to occur. These are picked up and amplified by the pendulum to produce this astonishing effect.

The point is that, when you are faced with a constantly changing situation, making time to focus on what success will look like for you can – and will – work.

A matter of life or death

Sociologist David Phillips of the University of California has spent his career proving that making your thoughts work for you rather than against you can even be a matter of life or death. Dr Phillips has studied whether people are able to postpone their death until after a moment of important emotional significance, which they are able to visualise. There is plenty of evidence to support this notion. For example, Charles M. Schulz, the multi-millionaire cartoonist and creator of *Peanuts*, died on the eve of the publication of his last comic strip, which contained a farewell letter signed by Schulz himself. Also, no fewer than three American presidents, John Adams, Thomas Jefferson and James Monroe, died on 4 July, thus raising the intriguing possibility that they all held on long enough to ensure an auspicious and patriotic date of death. Phillips examined whether people are more likely to die directly after a national holiday, like Christmas or Easter. He chose to study the Chinese Harvest Moon Festival, an event which takes place at a different time every year. This highly traditional celebration involves the senior woman of a household being helped by her daughters to prepare an elaborate family meal.

An examination of death records around the event showed that the death rate among the Chinese community dropped by 35 per cent from the average in the week before the festival, then rose by the same figure above the average the week after the celebrations, supporting the idea that our thoughts are powerful enough to allow us to postpone our demise, at least for a little while. This understanding inspired Sir Alex Ferguson to prolong a career long after most of his contemporaries, many of them younger men, had settled into retirement. 'My father retired on his sixty-fifth birthday, and one year later he was dead,' Ferguson said. 'The worst you can do is put your slippers on. People say things like: "I've worked for forty-five years. I have the right to rest." Not at all.' When he did finally announce his retirement in May 2013, he employed the same approach to his life outside of management as he did to his job. The journalist Charlie Rose enquired whether he had a 'bucket list', using the shorthand term for an inventory of things to do before you die. 'Yes, of course,' came the immediate response. 'I am all about looking forward.'

Horse racing is only part of the mental picture Ferguson painted of what retirement would look like. 'I'll travel more and I'll even read history books,' he revealed. 'I'll study new languages. I did four years of German at school. It comes easy with the guttural accent of the Scots. I've been studying French for years. I could take on Italian ... I already know a few sentences ...' So much to do and so little time.

Visions of change

Let's consider for a moment what sort of visualisation you could use to help you cope with change. Do you see yourself making a mistake at work? Do you ever imagine it all going wrong and you being left to dissect the errors you've made? These debilitating thoughts will not help you to deal with the demands of a situation whose outcome is of real importance to you. You simply must visualise success. So how do you do it?

First try this simple exercise.

Using the index finger on your writing hand, trace the capital letter 'Q' on your forehead. Make a mental note of how you did this.

Some people draw the letter so they can read it themselves. That is, they place the tail of the Q on the right-hand side of their forehead. Seen face on, it would look like this:

Other people draw the letter in the way that can be read by someone facing them, with the tail of the Q on the left-hand side of their forehead. Like this:

This quick test gives an insight into a measure known as self-monitoring. High self-monitors tend to draw the letter Q in the second way, which could be read by someone facing them. Low self-monitors tend to draw the letter Q so it could be read by themselves (the first example). Now, before all you high self-monitors start to get too smug and pat yourselves on the back, I must point out that this test also indicates that you are better liars too.

So, what does this have to do with the successful visualisation of dealing with change? This answer is that we all have an individual style and this test indicates which style you naturally use. Low self-monitors prefer to visualise from an internal perspective. This means that when they create a picture in their mind, it is from the perspective of what they see through their own eyes. It is as though someone has attached a camera to your head and you are broadcasting the images you can see. This internal perspective is often preferred by those who 'feel' what success will be like. Wayne Rooney prefers this approach. 'I see myself in situations where I'm in front of goal. My first touch is perfect; I'm getting a shot off at goal. It flies past the keeper,' is the way he describes his technique.

In contrast, high self-monitors visualise from an external perspective, which creates a picture in the mind similar to watching yourself on a TV screen. Ferguson's favourite footballing son, Cristiano Ronaldo, preferred this approach and used to describe the time he would spend visualising as 'going to the movies'. This external perspective is often thought to be useful for those who focus on seeing the images of success.

We are all able to switch between these styles of internal and external visualisation, but just as we have a preferred writing hand, we also have a natural visualising style, as demonstrated by the 'Q' exercise. It is important to emphasise that there is no right or wrong approach, because with regular practice you can develop the ability to use both inside and outside perspectives.

Try it with this next exercise and then assess for yourself which is the most effective approach for you.

- First, stand up and raise your right arm, pointing it forward in front of you.
- Now, keeping your arm outstretched, move it backwards to behind your body, twisting your waist as you do so. Move your arm as far you can, and see how far around your body it goes. It helps to pick a specific spot on the wall which indicates how far you have reached.
- With your arms by your sides, close your eyes, and imagine you are repeating the same movement. This time, in your mind 'see' your arm reach the point it reached before, and then easily, effortlessly and automatically, see it going another six, nine, maybe twelve inches further.
- Open your eyes and repeat it for real and feel that arm stretch further than it did before.

Now you know what it feels like to be Cristiano Ronaldo.

As we have said, those who thrive in changing times are able to see, feel and experience success before they ever actually achieve it. A formula to express this would be:

$$I \times V = R$$
Imagination × Vividness = Reality

You need to use your imagination to identify what you want and then get the picture really clear. The secret however is the '×' symbol in the middle, which means repetition and practice. Aristotle said that 'we are what we repeatedly do,' and he is right. Repetition really is the essence of all skills.

The Cantona test

Mozart, who began playing the piano at just three years old, estimated that 3,000 hours of determined practice could turn a novice into a decent player. In other words, practising for an average of two hours, six days a week for five years. The great composer also claimed that 10,000 hours' practice would allow you to reach the standard of a professional concert player, whilst ten years' constant practice and repetition would allow you to become a world-class musician.

Mozart's theory is still being applied in modern-day music conservatoires. It is a simple method that holds true: students who have practised for 10,000 hours or more tend to become professional concert performers. Those with 5,000 hours' practice become teachers.

The Mozart Test is echoed by a story about Eric Cantona – the man once referred to in an *Independent* newspaper headline as 'Bravura Cantona, the conductor of United cantata' – which Ferguson often used as an example to young players. The then French national coach, Gérard Houllier, had offered advice to Ferguson about managing Cantona: 'He likes to train and also he needs to train hard.'

At the end of his first United training session, as his team-mates were vanishing from the pitch, the Frenchman approached his manager and asked if he could have the assistance of two players.

'What for?' Ferguson asked.

'To practise,' he replied.

'That took me aback,' admitted Ferguson. 'It was not exactly a standard request but I was naturally delighted to accede to Eric's wishes.'

Meanwhile, the players who had gone indoors were realising that Cantona had not come back in and began to explore why. 'At the end of training the next day, several of them hung around to join in the practice with Eric and it soon became an integral part of my regime,' Ferguson explained. 'Nothing he did in matches meant more than the way he opened my eyes to the indispensability of practice. Practice makes players.'

It also makes great visualisers. As with any kind of training, you can carry out visualising your success with varying degrees of quality. If you follow the ideas below, you'll give yourself the best possible chance of making it effective. Remember, the more you use your skills, the better you will become.

1 Warm up

Warming up helps to make sure that you know exactly why you are going to use visualisation and how long you are going to spend doing it. Once you are prepared, you can start identifying the images which you need to play through your mind. Having identified these pictures, you can also make sure that you add the right level of feeling and vividness to them.

Before you start, make sure that you find a place where you will not be interrupted. Initially, it is hard to maintain concentration levels, so try to avoid distractions. Eventually, you will be able to cope with distractions as you get better at it. Choosing the right place to practice is important as there are many subtle factors which can have an influence on your performance.

When you are ready to start, choose a position which allows you to get the best possible pictures. This might be standing up or sitting down, but experiment by using different positions until you find one that suits you. For example, bobsleigh riders often find that they can only visualise effectively when they are sitting in the same position as when they are riding. Then, close your eyes and focus on getting your body in a state that you associate with the scenario in which you want to succeed – try to be as tension free as possible whilst remaining alert, focused and as ready as if it was a real-life scenario. Spend a minute or so getting into the right state of mind. Once there, your body and mind should be switched on to visualise the chosen context of your session.

Finally, if you need it, use this one last warm-up exercise. Close your eyes and imagine a friend. Try to get a sharp image of this person by visualising details: their hair, face colour, muscle structure and mannerisms. Now image this person talking. Imagine the sound and quality of their voice. Imagine their facial expressions. Think about how you feel about this person as they talk. Check out your emotions. Are they feelings of love, respect, anger, intimacy, trust? You can repeat this exercise until you are relaxed and ready to imagine the change scenario you face.

2 *Use all the senses … but feel it!*

Some senses are more relevant than others, but it seems that sound can be particularly important. This would certainly be the case for helping to bring the emotional side of the visualisation to the fore – for example, if football players can imagine the crowd noise or the sound of the perfectly struck shot, this can help make their images very vivid and emotionally charged. This is one of the major factors which inhibited many of Manchester United's opponents whilst Ferguson was manager. Old Trafford has long attracted the biggest crowds in the UK and enormous media interest. Many opponents coming to play United have failed to factor in the background noise of crowds, television cameras and other sounds which Ferguson's players took for granted. This has often upset their own vision of beating United.

It may also seem obvious to suggest, but you should visualise in colour. This is an important part of the content because as the control of your vision improves, the quality of the pictures will also improve and the colours will become sharper, thus making the whole image more realistic. I would encourage the use of all the senses but the kinaesthetic element, or *feel*, is probably more important than any other. The quality of the feelings can be assisted by concentrating on smaller details such as your movements. It may also be helpful to feel the kind of clothes you are wearing as these sort of details really help the brain recall images from within its memory stores, which helps to create a picture of the highest possible quality.

3 *Real time*

Visualising in real time is very important. Go through the scenario you have chosen to visualise at the same speed that it would happen if you were actually experiencing it. Cristiano Ronaldo's visualisation skills were once tested by having him practise headers in a pitch-black room. When the director of a documentary on the Portuguese player announced: 'No lights, camera, action!' night-vision technology showed that Ronaldo, in total darkness, was able to judge where a moving ball was going. 'I have to try to "see" the trajectory of a cross and put the ball in the net,' he said.

Some athletes are able to visualise their performance to within a fraction of a second, so their mind is being prepared as realistically as possible to face the real-life situation. Going through the visualisation too slowly will not give you the full benefit as your decision-making, movement patterns and reaction times are not being considered in a reliable way. Ronaldo 'scored' three times in succession, including a diving header.

Visualising in real time is not as easy as it sounds, so make sure you take it seriously. Practise by trying this simple task. Visualise yourself walking along a familiar route, maybe from the car park at work to your desk. Time how long this takes you when you visualise it and then the next time you take this route for real, check the actual time. I think you will be surprised by the results.

4 Quality sessions – set yourself goals

You should build up the length of your sessions little by little in order to get the best quality pictures for as long as possible. If you carry on for too long you will lose the quality of the visualisation and the session will lose its impact. Setting yourself time limits and focusing on doing shorter but more frequent sessions will help. Also, rate each session out of ten and assess the clarity, the quality and the control of each attempt you make. Most people find it difficult to stick to this routine. It is, however, an essential part of the survival kit for change.

Paul Hayward, Ferguson's ghost-writer, recounts how on the thirty-minute drive to the training ground, the manager would problem-solve. 'He prides himself on being able to think four moves ahead and this is an important period of his day,' Hayward says.

However, let's leave the last word on this to the man who claimed to be the greatest of all time, Muhammad Ali, the former world heavyweight boxing champion.

Muhammad Ali's use of visualisation is the stuff of legend. When he burst onto the world boxing scene, he was the first sportsman who started to make bold predictions concerning which round he was going to win his bout in. He would confidently declare his chosen route to victory in poems and rhymes. He made nineteen public predictions and was correct on seventeen occasions. He told me that he rehearsed his fights over and over in his head before he ever stepped into the ring. Ali won his 1969 comeback fight in Atlanta by knocking out Jerry Quarry in the third round. A local lawyer, Robert Kassell, was standing next to Ali's trainer, Angelo Dundee, when Dundee cut the laces of Ali's gloves after the victory. 'He peeled back the part that's below the hand,' Kassell recalled, 'and inside, written in ballpoint pen, it said, "Ali. KO, third round."'

Ali summed up the importance of practising visualisation by saying: 'Seeing your success is important because the fight is won or lost far away from witnesses. It is won behind the lines, in the gym and out there on the road, long before I ever dance under those lights.' He was talking about the cumulative effects of training on both your head and body. He knew that to get to the top, as well as hours and hours of hard physical work, you have to undergo disciplined mental rehearsal.

Change Your Focus

I'll tell you what I want, what I really, really want.

The Spice Girls

One of Sir Alex Ferguson's great strengths as Manchester United manager was to ensure that everyone at his club shared his ruthless focus on ignoring what he called 'the peripherals of change', and managing the challenge of focusing exclusively on being the best. His players still marvel at his capacity to make sure that wherever they were, all of them believed he knew exactly what they were up to, even if he didn't. It ensured that they would refuse to be swayed by the many distractions available to them. Mercurial Irish defender Paul McGrath recounts that during his regular nights out in the late 1980s, he would imagine Ferguson plotting his progress on an A–Z map of Manchester. 'Which is just as well,' he laughs, 'as more often than not, I was in no fit state to know where I was.'

Ferguson explained his reasoning: 'I can't have my players out doing commercial things every day, such as opening shops and doing charity things. These things are distractions from winning. They must maintain their focus on the main thing.

'A lack of focus uses energy, which is so vital,' he continued. 'Someone needs to be in control of that. Someone *has* to be in control of that.' The importance of this philosophy is best illustrated through case studies of two of his most celebrated players, Ryan Giggs and David Beckham.

During the Easter period of 1992, the hectic final ten days of the race for the Championship were causing Alex Ferguson frustration. His team were in the process of throwing away their best chance since 1967 of winning the League, following a dismal defeat at West Ham United, which came just two days after a 2–1 home reverse to Brian Clough's Nottingham Forest on Easter Monday. The day after the disappointment at Upton Park, Ferguson attended an English Schools Football Association function in Morecambe, where a fellow diner mentioned he had seen Lee Sharpe and Ryan Giggs out clubbing in Blackpool just hours after the Forest defeat and less than two days before they were due to face West Ham. Ferguson left the dinner as soon as he could politely get away, and described himself as 'having steam coming out of my ears' whilst heading south back to Manchester, still dressed in his bow tie and dinner jacket.

Ferguson said: 'I drove straight to Sharpe's house and had to park about thirty yards up the street because of the number of cars outside his door. Music was blasting out from the house. When the door was opened to me, I burst in with all guns blazing. There was a full-scale party going on and there must have been about twenty people in the place, including Giggs and three young apprentices.

'It was the presence of those boys that detonated my temper and I went berserk. I ordered everybody out of the house and as each apprentice passed I gave him a cuff on the back of the head.' The comic thing, according to Giggs's then girlfriend, Joanna Fairhurst, is that 'he didn't call the players by name. He just yelled "ELEVEN!" and "FIVE!", and ordered them to join him in the living room.' Eleven and five were Giggs's and Sharpe's respective shirt numbers.

Giggs recalls the terrifying moment when he was caught bang to rights by an incandescent Ferguson: 'I opened Sharpey's door, I was holding a Becks beer and there was no escape for me.' Some other, unidentified trainees did escape via various routes, including a window, once they heard the unmistakable tones of the man they called 'gaffer'. Sharpe, who had bought the house not long before, was still upstairs getting ready when he was summoned to the lounge for a dressing down. Ferguson said: 'My anger was directed more at Lee than Ryan because there had been other signs of waywardness in Lee's off-field behaviour.' Sharpe later recalled how Ferguson instructed him to get rid of everything – including his house and girlfriend – and go back to lodging with a landlady. He was sold to Leeds United four years later and his career never reached the heights which his talent had once promised. Joanna Fairhurst recalls that Ferguson threatened to phone the player's mother. 'When I spoke to Ryan the next day, he said he had been fined a month's wages.'

The stinging rebuke certainly worked on Giggs, who continued playing for United beyond his fortieth birthday, setting the record for the number of club appearances, and becoming world football's most decorated player. Ferguson said: 'I have never had any bother from Ryan since that incident. He has developed into a fine young man and I have become very proud of him over the years.'

Giggs acknowledged the impact of Ferguson's warning to him to avoid distractions: 'In later years, you'd go out on a Saturday night and he'd tell you where you were, what you'd done and who you were with. You'd think, "How does he know that?" He just knew everyone. If I came here for training clean shaven, he'd say I'd been out the night before.' Giggs joked that he stopped shaving when he went out, but he would also take his responsibilities seriously. In contrast, David Beckham chose to dismiss his manager's advice.

Ferguson says: 'David was the only player I managed who chose to be famous, who made it his mission to be known outside the game.' This contrasts with other prodigies such as Wayne Rooney, who 'had commercial offers that would make your mind boggle', and Giggs, who heeded the lessons to avoid the siren call of 'the corporate world that would love to have taken him over ... he learned and that was never his style.' Both have taken on commercial commitments, but neither has let anything come before football.

Beckham has fond memories of the first time he met Ferguson, back in the late 1980s, when he was in his early teens and Ferguson was trying to persuade him he should commit his future to the club. United were in London, preparing to play Crystal Palace, and the thirteen-year-old Beckham was taken to the Travelodge where they were staying. Ferguson introduced Beckham to United icons Bryan Robson and Steve Bruce. He let him help the kit man, Norman Davies, clear up in the United dressing room after the game. He took him to a pre-match meal with the players and watched in amusement as the schoolboy ordered a salmon steak, thinking it was just a variety of steak, never imagining it was fish.

Ferguson knew Beckham's name. He regularly telephoned his parents, Ted and Sandra. He even allowed him to sit on the bench during a game against West Ham United at Upton Park. 'Ferguson was everything to me,' Beckham admitted. 'He was the pathway to my dreams.'

Ferguson kept a paternal eye on him when Beckham moved from Essex to Manchester at just fifteen, and admired the youngster's dedication and focus during his rise through the great United youth team of 1992. In the summer of 1995, he ignored the former Liverpool defender turned television pundit Alan Hansen's assertion that 'You don't win anything with kids,' and resisted the temptation to buy a big-name player, preferring to give Beckham his chance.

Ferguson first began to express concerns about Beckham's focus when the footballer met Spice Girl Victoria Adams, whom he married in 1999. 'After training he'd always be practising, practising, practising. But his life changed when he met his wife. He developed this "fashion thing" and I could see his transition to a different person,' lamented the Scot. This created a tension, and despite Gary Neville's intervention as a mediator between manager and player following a number of disagreements – after which Beckham agreed to a list of commitments which included not travelling to London in the three days preceding a game – Ferguson remained unconvinced.

Club legend Sir Bobby Charlton noticed that 'Apart from his wonderful ball skills, Beckham also had another extremely well-developed talent: understanding the way publicity works, how it is that an image is made. That is a skill David Beckham no doubt honed as he travelled through his wife's celebrity world.'

Charlton recounts watching a game at Old Trafford around the time it seemed that Beckham's lifestyle was beginning to take over from his football: 'Someone leaned over and whispered in my ear, "Have you noticed what David Beckham does when he scores? He runs to the corner flag all on his own. If someone else scores, he's usually the first one hanging on him. I suppose it means he is always in the picture."'

Ferguson had already spotted it and knew the dangers. 'You should never surrender what you're good at,' he warned. 'David's eye was off the ball which was a real shame because if he had maintained his focus he would have been one of the greatest Manchester United legends.' Instead, in an acrimonious departure, Beckham was sold to Real Madrid in 2003.

Given Ferguson's assertion that a Spice Girl was a significant factor in David Beckham's exit from Manchester United, let's refer to the power of focus working on 'The Spice Girls Principle' – the more you want and focus on something, the more of it you get.

Take a few moments to think about what actually happens to your focus when you are under the pressures of change. Do you become so completely focused on your performance that nothing else matters? Or are you easily distracted?

By the way, think about what you want to achieve by reading this chapter. Is there something more important you could be doing? Is there anything else which is going on in your life right now which needs your immediate attention? Are you sure that you didn't leave the oven on before you left the house today?

Have I now distracted you from the purpose of reading this chapter?

If you have tried to answer the questions above, then I have successfully shifted your focus around, so it has not necessarily been where you wanted it to be. You may have been focused, but not necessarily focused on the things that will help. This is what can happen to your focus when faced with change. There are lots of things fighting for your attention and it becomes difficult to keep it directed on what really matters.

Standing room only

Sir Alex Ferguson was once asked: 'If the average coach says 100 words to his players, how many words should a great coach say?' Ferguson let the questioner know he had really heard the question and was giving it due consideration. He placed a friendly hand on their shoulder and delivered a simple response.

'Ten words,' he said. 'Fewer, if possible.'

The truth is, great coaches and teachers don't spend their time talking. They spend most of their time watching and listening. And when they communicate, they don't just start talking. They deliver concise, useful information, and they make that information stick. Just like Ferguson did when he communicated his answer.

Andy Cole remembers one occasion when just eight words from his manager were sufficient.

'We played Tottenham Hotspur and they destroyed us in the first half, leading 3–0 at the break,' Cole explains. 'I expected a furious manager to rip into us but instead, he sat on a chair and folded his arms. Then he didn't speak for fifteen minutes. He let the players argue and debate among themselves while he just listened.

'The manager's reaction spooked us a bit. When the referee blew his whistle for the teams to go out for the second half, Ferguson stood up and simply said, "I think you know how to rectify this."' United scored five second-half goals to win 5–3.

The problem with our focus is that there is simply not enough of it to go around. It doesn't let you deal with everything that's demanding your full attention. Your conscious mind has a limited capacity and is only able to hold a relatively small amount of information at any one time. This is why telephone numbers are traditionally seven digits long. We can comfortably store only seven bits of information at a time; after that we start forgetting things in order to house new ones. You have probably had the experience of hearing a clock chime the hour, then afterwards asking yourself how many times it struck. Up to seven chimes and we can recall the sound; after that, we have no chance. When we try to remember information that contains more than seven things, we naturally break it down into smaller chunks. For example, a line of poetry that contains more than seven beats needs to be broken into two lines.

Read the following string of numbers quickly and only once, then look away and write them down on a sheet of paper in the same order they appear below.

7   2   0   9   6   3   1   4   8   5

How many did you get right?

The chances are you will have got at least one wrong. Remembering ten numbers in the correct order overloads your conscious mind. Even if you did write them down in the correct order, you would not have been able to think about anything else whilst you were doing it, because the space is so limited. It follows, then, that when you face change, what you put or allow into your mind is extremely important. This means getting rid of unhelpful thoughts and replacing them with more useful ones. For example, keeping worries or doubts in there is a waste of space as they are unlikely to help you successfully cope with change. They need to be banished to allow space for more useful thoughts.

Let's look at ways to do this.

The Doctor Who principle

Dr Philip Zimbardo, a highly respected psychologist, believes that we can target our focus in three directions:

- the past
- the present
- the future

He suggests that whilst our thoughts can travel in all three directions, problems start to occur when we allow ourselves to become fixated on one perspective. Instead, we must follow the lead of another doctor, the fictional timelord Doctor Who, and have a flexible time-perspective.

Past

In Disney's *The Lion King*, Rafiki, the wise old baboon, tries to persuade Simba to return home and save his pride. Simba, who believes that he is responsible for the death of his father, refuses because he thinks people won't understand. Rafiki looks at him and tells him that his father's death is in the past and he must move on. Simba says that he can't. Rafiki then takes the stick that he carries around with him and hits Simba on the head. Simba roars in pain and asks why he did it. Rafiki looks at him, shrugs and says, 'It doesn't matter; it's in the past!' Then he takes another swipe, but this time Simba is waiting and ducks to avoid the blow. Rafiki laughs and says, 'The way I see it, you can either run from the past or you can learn from it.'

Sir Alex Ferguson was not adverse to using this same tactic – of reminding his players about their place within the context of the history of the club – to shift their mindset. In the run-up to the fiftieth anniversary of the Munich air disaster, he invited Sir Bobby Charlton, an Old Trafford director who had survived the plane crash, to address the squad. Ferguson said that it was 'possible to hear a pin drop' as an emotional Charlton paid tribute to the twenty-three people, including eight of his playing colleagues and three members of the club's staff, who had died when a plane carrying Sir Matt Busby's team crashed off the runway at Munich airport on 6 February 1958.

Following this meeting, defender Rio Ferdinand said he now understood how Munich was 'the starting point, really, for the tradition, the start of setting down the standard for Manchester United Football

Club'. Charlton explained, 'It was not intended to put pressure on them. They have their own careers and Munich is a long time ago, but it was Matt Busby who pioneered the idea of English clubs competing in Europe and the Babes, who would have done so well in it but for the tragedy, set standards which are worth remembering.' As well as listening to Charlton's speech, the players were given specially made DVDs to educate them about what had happened in Munich. 'The history is not lost on these players now,' said Charlton. 'All of them who come here sometimes get a little puzzled by the effect what happened in Munich has had on Manchester United. But when the club asked me to talk to the players about Munich and the effect it had on United, they understood it and were fascinated by it.' Just a few months later, those same players won the European Cup, beating Chelsea in a Moscow downpour. Ferguson decreed that Charlton lead the players up to collect the trophy.

Although learning lessons from the past is useful, spending too much mental time there can be fatal to your chances of dealing with the immediate challenges of change. I once worked with a tennis player who spent a lot of time beating himself up for the mistakes he had made in a game. I asked him what happened if he started a game thinking about the previous match. He shrugged, and so to make the point, when he began his practice session, I physically jumped on his back.

Although I felt ridiculous, he got the message. When we spend our time thinking too much about the past instead of the present, it can only have the same effect of slowing us down.

The golfer Ian Woosnam made a similar mistake during the 2001 British Open. He had just taken the lead on the final day, when his caddie, Miles Byrne, told him that he had accidentally forgotten to count how many clubs Woosnam had in his bag. He was carrying too many, which would cost him two shots by way of official sanction. Despite incurring this penalty, it still left Woosnam in the lead. Then he did what most of us do and focused his mind on the past. For the next five holes his mind was there rather than on the actual game and he lost his lead. He eventually finished in third place, which cost him £230,000 in prize money. Ferguson suggests that 'Sometimes playing well is about mastering the art of forgetting the past.'

Present

> *Carpe Diem. Quam minimum credula postero. (Seize the day; put no trust in tomorrow.)*
>
> Horace

We have already seen how limited our focus is and how having lots of things competing for our attention can stop us from coping with change. For the most part, these distractions tend to be predictable in that they come with the territory. For example, in sport they include crowd noise, poor refereeing decisions and an opponent trying to psych you out. The equivalent at work will be more specific to your own circumstances but may include continual interruptions by colleagues, emails that need a reply and a never-ending list of phone calls to return.

Former United midfielder Roy Keane, a man whose own intense focus is the stuff of legend, admired Ferguson's ability to keep his players focused on the immediate task facing them. 'He radiates purpose. He's intense, focused, driven,' Keane marvelled, before their well-publicised fallout. 'It never ceases to amaze me, especially on the days when the carnival atmosphere around the place can cause you to forget the objective.' Ferguson's favourite method of ensuring that focus was absolute was a simple reminder he would deliver when standing at the dressing-room door. He would look every player in the eye and shake their hand whilst asking them to 'Remember who you are, remember that you are Manchester United players. Remember what you did to get here, now go and do it one more time. And you'll win.'

When Andy Murray won his first Wimbledon tennis title in 2013, he told reporters that a long conversation with Ferguson had helped him deal with the pressure of becoming the first British man to triumph at the All

England Club for seventy-seven years. Murray, who described the advice as 'gold dust', said that Ferguson told him that his teams were built on consistency and concentration. 'If you can concentrate and focus for the entire match,' Ferguson advised his fellow Scot, 'the consistency will follow.'

His advice was similar to that used by the tennis legend Billie Jean King when she helped Martina Navratilova cope with distractions and return her focus on the 1982 Wimbledon tennis final by 'getting her mind into the now'. Before the game, Navratilova's focus had started to slip into the past (worrying about previous failures) and into the future (what the consequences of a defeat would mean) before Billie Jean brought her back into the now by asking her to describe the wallpaper in the changing room. Billie Jean explained: 'This forced her to focus on the imme-diate details of her environment and so, when she was playing, she used this same simple trick to help herself stay focused on the game.'

The present is the state that athletes are referring to when they talk about being in the zone. Think again about your best performance, the one that you recalled in the introductory chapter. You remembered an occasion when you were performing at your very best. I'll bet that when you were in this moment, your mind was in the present.

To learn how to focus on the now, try this exercise.

Become intensely aware of your breathing. Count the breaths you take. *One … two … three … four … five.* Repeat the exercise. Do it again. Keep counting. It seems like a simple task, but eventually your mind begins to wander. If your mind isn't focused on your breathing, make a note of what it is that distracted you. Focusing on your breathing helps you to control the direction of your focus. The women's marathon world record holder, Paula Radcliffe, does a similar exercise to ensure that she keeps her attention in the here and now of a race. 'I count to 100 three times – that's a mile. That's how I count the miles off. I think about the minute I'm in now rather than what's left to come.'

When change is happening all around you, you too must be fully present. The comedienne Joan Rivers sums it up:

> *Yesterday is history.*
> *Tomorrow is a mystery.*
> *Today is what counts.*
> *That's why we call it the present.*

Future

David Beckham and his team-mates were sitting in the dressing room at Manchester United's Carrington training centre when in walked the club's sports psychologist, Bill Beswick. He proceeded to recount a tale which fired the players' imagination into the future and fuelled their desire to create something special in the name of Manchester United. Beswick told them a story of three men who were laying bricks. Each was asked what he was doing. 'Laying bricks,' answered the first. 'Earning £10 per hour,' replied the second. The third was driven by a bigger vision and said: 'I'm building a cathedral and, one day, I'll bring my kids back here and tell them that their dad contributed to this magnificent building.'

Beswick suggested to Beckham and his team-mates that they could apply these three approaches to the training session they were about to embark on. 'I'm just practising,' would be the answer from the first player training. 'I'm earning £1,000 per hour,' would be the second. The third response would be: 'I'm helping to build the best Manchester United team ever and I'll be proud to tell my grandchildren I was part of it.' Still pondering Beswick's words, Beckham and company commenced training. Beckham promptly scored a gem from thirty yards and ran off in celebration, shouting, 'Cathedral Builders 1, Bricklayers 0.'

Economists use the term Social Discount Rate (SDR) to describe the value we place on the future. Your SDR is an important indicator regarding your ability to cope with change. Psychologists have carried out tests to highlight this point. In one experiment, unsupervised four-year-old children were told that if they could wait for fifteen minutes before eating a marshmallow, they would be rewarded with a second one. Significantly, when researchers revisited these once tiny research participants as teenagers some fourteen years later, those who had held on for the second marshmallow were found to be better able to deal with life's frustrations than the more impulsive children. How could a simple test, of waiting for a treat, prove this? Well, it appears that if you didn't know how to anticipate the benefits of the future and resist a marshmallow at age four, it seems you were unlikely to have learned to see the benefits of investing time to study for exams at age eighteen.

If you want to start recognising whether you are someone who spends too much time focusing on the future, check whether you are a resident of Someday Isle. It's a place where you can do so much when you eventually get there ...

Someday Isle ... write a book
Someday Isle ... leave my job
Someday Isle ... ask for a pay rise

One of my favourite pieces of writing to capture the essence of this point is written by 89-year-old Nadine Stair.

If I had my life over I'd make more mistakes this time. I would relax. I would limber up and would be sillier than I have been on this trip. I know of very few things that I would take seriously. I would laugh more and cry less. I would be crazier. I would worry less about what others thought of me and would accept myself as I am. I would climb more mountains, swim in more rivers and watch more sunsets. I would eat more ice cream and fewer beans. I would watch TV less and have more picnics. I would only have actual troubles and very few imaginary ones. I would feel only sad not depressed. I would be concerned not anxious. I would be annoyed not angry. I would regret mistakes but not feel guilty about them.

I would tell more people that I liked them. I would touch my friends. I would forgive others for being human and would hold no grudges. I would play with more children and listen to more old people. I would go after what I wanted without believing I needed it and I wouldn't place such great value on money.

You see I am one of those people who lived cautiously and sensibly and sanely, hour after hour, day after day. Oh, I have had my moments and if I had to do it over again I'd have more of them. In fact I would have nothing else. Just moments, one after another, instead of living so many years ahead of each day. I have been one of those people who never go anywhere without a thermometer, a hot water bottle, a gargle, a raincoat and a parachute. If I had to do it over again, I would go places and do things and travel lighter than I have. I would plant more seeds and make the world more beautiful. I would express my feelings of love without fear.

If I had my life to live over, I would start bare footed earlier in the spring and stay that way until later in the fall. I would play hooky more. I would ride on more merry-go-rounds. I'd pick more daisies and I would smile because I would be living free.

Don't wait until you're eighty-nine years old before you begin recognising the importance of your focus. Rather than let the direction of it become an unconscious habit, you should actively develop a flexible time-perspective in which you can invest your full attention in whichever direction is going to be most helpful. Our mind is like Doctor Who's Tardis, a time machine that we must learn to use wisely.

When coping with change, how else can you ensure that your focus is concentrated on the things that really matter? Here are three more simple ideas to help you.

1 Accept the existence of distractions

Distractions are a natural part of your environment; they exist and there is very little you can do about them. Don't try to ignore them, because the effort that this involves uses up some of your valuable and limited focus.

So how do you deal with them?

2 Recognise distractions – identify what matters

Take the time to recognise the distractions that can upset you.

England defender Paul Parker recalls one particular incident when this lesson was learned with dramatic effect: 'We returned to the dressing room at half-time in one game which we were losing. The manager was not happy, especially as someone's mobile phone was ringing. It was at a time when everyone had a similar ringtone so everyone was hoping it wasn't their phone.' A very nervous Steve Bruce answered his phone and switched it off almost immediately. The manager grabbed the phone as Bruce explained that he needed to keep it on as his wife was in hospital, having an operation on her bad back. 'I know four bad backs,' screamed Ferguson. 'Four bad defenders at the back.' With that, he smashed Bruce's phone on the floor.

One different – and less expensive – approach is to apply a traffic light metaphor, such as that used by Sir Steve Redgrave and his gold medal-winning colleagues before he achieved his unprecedented fifth consecutive Olympic rowing title. They brainstormed all of the possible distractions which might cost them victory. They then posted these on a list and ticked them off whenever they occurred in training, which proved to be an amusing game rather than a distraction. The group then asked one another whether these distractions could beat them. They agreed that they couldn't. Having done so, they asked what colour would best describe their self-control if they did allow distractions to get the better of them. They answered that they would see red. If they stayed in perfect control and progressed smoothly, then instead they would see green. They also agreed that amber was the moment of decision, when they could choose to either return to green or go to red. Throughout the Olympic tournament, the team would then have a standard call to 'stay in the green', whenever they felt that a distraction was going to force them to lose focus.

What are the things that can derail you? Make a list of them and decide how you will deal with them.

3 Am I focusing on what really matters?

This simple question acts as an effective trigger to help you re-focus on the things that matter. Some senior managers at one company I work with have small notes with the question 'Am I focusing on what really matters?' stuck on items they frequently use, like phones and computer screens. These reminders act as a trigger to recognise where their focus has wandered to.

This is similar to the advice Ferguson dispensed to Tony Blair's press secretary, Alastair Campbell, who asked him in 2001 how to handle the pressures of a gruelling UK General Election. 'You have to be ruthless,' Ferguson said. 'Put the blinkers on. Don't let anyone into your space unless you want them there. If someone says only you can deal with it, give them a few seconds and if you decide someone else can solve it, move on.'

Another effective solution is to have a transition zone. The coaches at Manchester United do this to help their players block off distractions from their home life and focus on playing football. They draw a white line about ten yards behind the training pitches. The area behind the line is the 'thinking zone'. In the thinking zone, the players receive feedback from the coaches about the aims of the session. Once they have figured out what they want to do, they cross the line into the 'play zone'. Before they cross the line, the players must begin focusing on the session and forget any distractions. The coaches start the session with an exercise which requires the players to keep possession of the ball. As each player arrives on the field, he must try to win the ball from the previous one. When this well-established routine has fully switched on all the players, the coaches know they are focused and ready for quality practice.

Your transition zone could be the time you spend in your car driving to work, or even the time before this when you are getting ready for the day ahead. When you get dressed, open your mental wardrobe. With each article of clothing you put on – shirt, belt, shoes – let go of a problem you are worried about. By the time you are changed, you'll have shed all your unhelpful distractions and personal concerns and be able to focus on dealing with the present.

The ING Bank in America uses this same idea outside its head office building, where a thick white line is painted directly in front of the entrance, and above the line is painted a question, aimed at the Bank's employees: 'DOES TODAY REALLY MATTER?' I have also seen something similar in factories, where a blue line has been drawn across the entrance to the doorway. There is a rule which states that once you have crossed the blue line, you cannot be thinking about yesterday's problems or daydreaming about tomorrow's challenges. Crossing the threshold means that your mind must be focused on your job and nothing else.

Now think of your own trigger which will stimulate you to ask the question, 'Am I focusing on what really matters?' Make a list of your ideas.

Change Your View

I've been waiting for this opportunity all of my life. I'm not thinking of fatigue. Fatigue is the clothes which the army wear.

Michael Jordan, before winning his first
NBA basketball title

Let's begin this chapter with a quiz.

Sir Alex Ferguson is often described as tyrannical, dictatorial and unforgiving, oozing the characteristics of fictional mob bosses such as Tony Soprano, a man with whom he shares certain 'qualities' such as an infamous temper and astute prudence. Read the quotations below and see if you can spot the difference between the Scot and the Soprano.

1. 'He was certainly full of it, calling me boss and big man.'

2. 'Not one of you can look me in the eye, because not one of you deserves to have a say.'
3. 'Those who want respect, give respect.'
4. 'All due respect, you got no fucking idea what it's like to be Number One. Every decision you make affects every facet of every other fucking thing.'
5. 'If you can quote the rules, then you can obey them.'
6. 'A wrong decision is better than indecision.'[1]

Whilst the quotes could easily have come from either mouth, it would do a disservice to Ferguson's deep understanding of human nature to suggest that his success as a manager was solely due to his ability to wield a proverbial sledgehammer. He possessed an acute ability to manage his outlook to deal with change.

At a UEFA football coaches conference, French coach Gérard Houllier once shared an insight into the myriad tasks an elite-level coach needs to carry out, and the demands made of him. He described the unrelenting pressures coaches face, stresses which eventually caused him to retire with heart problems. He said that his twenty-five years' experience had taught him a particularly valuable lesson: the importance of the five-minute rule. More specifically, 'The

---

1 The first three quotations are Ferguson's, the latter three from Tony Soprano.

five minutes after a game, when a manager stands in front of the cameras, are the most important five minutes of a manager's week, because the players, fans and your employers are watching for positive or negative signs.'

Two of Ferguson's great managerial rivals, Arsène Wenger and Jose Mourinho, concur. Mourinho calls it the 'second game', which is crucial as it offers an opportunity 'to start playing the next game before it starts'. Wenger suggests that 'This period of time is key because the image of the team is reflected in the manager's face. You can tell the manager who's under pressure.' To illustrate this, look at some less well known but equally important words, which Ferguson uttered in the five minutes following a setback, and which offer an illustration of his ability to manage his – and by default – his team's outlook.

'We have to recover, we have to be fast about it. In the history of Manchester United this is another day and we will recover.'

*May 1992, following United's failure
to win the first League title since 1967*

'That's in the past and I'm more interested in tomorrow. We've got to look forward now. There are big opportunities at this club and we have a lot of challenges ahead of us. You never go through a season where everything is rosy. When you get the bad moments you have to recover from it. The ability to do that is a tremendous credit to every player we've had here.'

May 1995, following the loss of the League title to Blackburn Rovers and the FA Cup final to Everton

'I don't like this, but we'll have to meet the challenge. We'll have to step up to the mark.'
May 2012, following Manchester City's title triumph

'That is part of the tapestry of Manchester United: the recovery. I always kept in mind that it was not all victories and open-top parades.'
May 2013

I like these quotes as they remind me of the influence our outlook can have, especially during times of change. It cannot be overestimated.

Managing your outlook can be done in three simple ways:

- using optimism
- looking for highlights
- gaining a sense of perspective

Let's look at each of them in turn.

Optimism

Optimism is the faith that leads to achievement. Nothing can be done without hope or confidence. No pessimist has ever discovered the secrets of the stars or sailed to uncharted lands or opened a new doorway for the human spirit.

Helen Keller, the first deaf and blind person to attend an American university

On the night before winning the 2008 Champions League final in Moscow against Chelsea, Ferguson arrived for the final press conference before the big match. Typically, these affairs are opportunities for managers to issue bland phrases straight from the handbook of managerial clichés. ('We're looking forward to it.' 'We'll do our best.') Journalist Daniel Taylor watched Ferguson step into the room and expected a typically anodyne affair. Instead, he noticed, 'his demeanour was more like a man arriving for a family barbeque than a manager on the cusp of his single most important match since the turn of the century.' Taylor and his colleagues watched in astonishment as 'He began the event by declaring, "I love you all," his eyes sparkling, spreading out his arms in the manner of the Pope. "I have come to spread peace," he laughed.' Taylor deadpans, 'It was not the usual way a manager would address an audience of journalists, television crews, photographers and blazer-wearing UEFA officials.' Yet this was Ferguson at his best: warm, charming, convivial and incredibly relaxed, especially given everything that was at stake. Particularly because of everything that was at stake.

'I feel good,' Ferguson volunteered when asked to describe his state of mind. And then he started to twitch his arms exaggeratedly. 'Apart from the shakes, of course …'

Professor Martin Seligman from the University of Pennsylvania is a world-renowned authority on positive psychology and has published a wealth of material on the subject. He would certainly approve of Ferguson's strategy. In his work, he uses a steady flow of scientific evidence to show that having an optimistic outlook on life has beneficial effects – not only does it help us deal with change but it boosts our immune system and improves our general mood. Dr Seligman shows that people with an optimistic outlook on life tend to be more motivated, more likely to persevere at challenges and, not surprisingly, more successful at coping with change in the long term.

One example he uses involves a study of over 2,000 Finnish men. After answering a series of questions, these men were classed as being pessimistic (they expected the future to be bleak), optimistic (they had higher expectations about the future) or neutral (their expectations were neither especially positive or negative). They were then monitored over a six-year period. It was found that the men in the pessimistic group were far more likely to die from cancer, cardiovascular disease and accidents than those in the neutral group, whilst those in the optimistic group exhibited a far lower mortality rate than either of the other two groups. This was a lesson which Ferguson had to learn the hard way.

He took an unprecedented month-long holiday in Malta to reflect on the loss of his first real chance, in 1992, to win United's first League title in a quarter of a century. Ferguson says: 'In those moments of defeat and acceptance, there would be a dawning, for me, of where we needed to go. My feeling was always: "I don't like this, but we'll have to meet the challenge. We'll have to step up to the mark." It wouldn't have been me or the club, to submit to apocalyptic thoughts about that being the end, the finish of all our work.' When he came back to the club, his message to both his players and the supporters was consistently optimistic. 'When we returned to pre-season training, Ferguson had a right go,' says Paul Parker. 'His message was loud and clear: no losers, no sulkers and make sure we don't fall again. We were already mentally stronger and filled with a collective determination to right the wrongs of the previous season.'

Ferguson gave the supporters the same message through the medium of his programme notes: 'The important thing is that we must not allow ourselves to think that Manchester United's failure to win the

League since 1967 is some kind of curse on the club. We must not sink into a slough of despondency, believing that the world is against us, because that way lies defeat and the possibility of submission.'

There are powerful examples from outside the world of football where a failure to be optimistic can also be fatal to coping with change. Compare the reactions of two chairmen of US airlines in the turbulent days immediately after the attacks on 11 September 2001, when the airline industry went into a state of panic.

American Airlines CEO Don Carty spoke to his employees about how the 'business's long and proud history would give a solid base for resolving our financial challenge'. He reminded his people of their company's long and distinguished history, including the gesture of giving half its fleet to the military in the Second World War to support the Allies, and invited them to draw their own inspiration from it. He then outlined a series of targets that the business had to achieve to continue operating. The trade unions described it as 'an incredibly galvanizing message' and it was the only US airline not to file for bankruptcy.

In comparison, United Airlines CEO James Goodwin issued a letter at the same time to all of his employees warning them that 'United Airlines is literally haemorrhaging money,' and lecturing that 'clearly if this bleeding continues, we will perish sometime next year.' Following this letter, the already declining stock price of the airline fell by a further 25 per cent before it was eventually forced to declare bankruptcy. Goodwin was sacked two weeks later.

It is easy to be cynical about this approach. Comedian Billy Connolly defined an optimist as 'someone who gets chased up a tree by a lion but still enjoys the scenery'. Yet it is a quality which attracts people. In the last twenty-four US presidential elections, American voters have chosen the candidate who is considered more naturally optimistic on nineteen occasions. I am not advocating being like Voltaire's Doctor Pangloss, who sees sunshine in every situation no matter how gloomy, but I am suggesting that you resist the natural temptation to find fault and assume the worst.

We all possess the ability to be optimistic. Psychologists call it 'affective forecasting'. Let me give you an example of how it works. Have you ever been about to buy a new outfit and convinced yourself that buying it will change your life, elevate your status among your neighbours and make you more appealing to members of the opposite sex? You believe that buying the new clothes will definitely bring you to a new level of contentment. You don't anticipate that the effect will quickly start to wear off. If you did, you probably wouldn't buy it, right? We regularly overestimate the impact that purchases like this will have on our lives. I think it proves, though, that we are naturally optimistic.

Therefore, when you are facing change, you should start to use this natural gift to your advantage.

Look at the two exercises below. In simple terms, they show that the way we think affects the way we feel, which in turn affects our behaviour. It therefore follows that if we wish to change our behaviour, we need to influence our feelings, which is best done by changing the way we think. For example, if we think pessimistically, it leads to negative feelings, resulting in low confidence and poor performance. In contrast, having an optimistic outlook leads to positive feelings, higher confidence and better performance. So, complete the two exercises and then reflect on how you can go about adopting a more optimistic outlook towards the change you face.

1. Identify three challenges you have faced when you displayed a negative and pessimistic outlook. Under the three headings, THOUGHTS – FEELINGS – BEHAVIOUR, make some notes describing the situation, how you felt and what impact it had on you.

2. Identify three challenges you have faced when you displayed a really positive and optimistic outlook. Make some notes, again under the headings THOUGHTS – FEELINGS – BEHAVIOUR, describing the situation, how you felt and what impact it had on you.

Highlights

The average person looks without seeing, listens without hearing, touches without feeling, eats without tasting, moves without physical awareness, inhales without awareness of odour or fragrance and talks without thinking.

Leonardo da Vinci

At the end of 1989, Manchester United fans had grown tired of the team's increasingly poor results and performances, even going so far as unfurling a banner which read, '3 years of excuses and it's still crap ... Ta ra Fergie!' Ferguson was forced to call it 'black December', when he reached 'the lowest, most desperate point ever in all my years in management'.

He went to see Sir Matt Busby, who puffed away on his pipe and asked how things were. Ferguson explained that he was having a hard time from the newspapers. 'And Sir Matt asked, "Why are you reading them?" That was the simplest advice anyone could possibly imagine and I couldn't even think of it myself,' Ferguson later admitted. Instead he chose to read the letters of support he received from colleagues and supporters. One letter in particular helped shift his bleak outlook.

Willie Muirhead, his old chairman from his first managerial job at East Stirlingshire, had written. He posed the question, 'Is this the same Alex Ferguson that I knew as a young lad that I presented with his first chance in management? The one I saw running full-pelt down the track towards a linesman in a rage? The one I had to haul back from any trouble? Is this the same man who is going to give in easy now at Manchester United?' The letter seemed to galvanise Ferguson. He promised the supporters that the 1990s would herald 'a decade of success at this club', a promise he kept with some style.

This experience, of looking for highlights in the midst of pressure, was an important technique which Ferguson subsequently employed with regularity. He would often stop his players and ask them a general knowledge question – for instance, how heavy is a football? – and if they got it right he'd ask them something else. 'Alex always loved a quiz and I remember one coach trip when Viv Anderson challenged him to name four England internationals with an "x" in their name,' recalls former England defender Mike Duxbury. 'He got Lee and Kerry Dixon and Graham Rix, but just couldn't get the fourth. There I was, sat right next to him on the coach thinking: "Thanks boss, that's just great!"'

At other times Ferguson and his coaches conducted quizzes for the youth players in his crammed office. 'Some of the answers they gave were absolutely hilarious,' youth team coach Eric Harrison laughs. 'It served an important role. The players realised they could relax in the company of the Boss.' Ferguson would pride himself on his ability to make his players and staff laugh, often using one of his barbed one-liners about an opponent or referee. 'That bloody ref,' he joked once. 'He runs like the hairs in his arse are tied together.' Having heard that the staff in the club's laundry team had accidentally broken environmental regulations by using bleach in their washing machines, Ferguson rang them up, putting on a fake, nasal accent and pretending to be from the local council: 'I wonder if you could explain to me why all the ducks in the nearby pond have disappeared.'

Canada's leading sports psychologist, Professor Terry Orlick, echoes Ferguson's philosophy and suggests a simple approach to achieving optimism:

> Life is full of extraordinary opportunities for embracing simple joys within ordinary experiences. Joyfulness lives within the magic of opening our minds and hearts to find joy in simplicity itself. Any occasion that can create feelings of intimacy, connection, worthiness, contribution, accomplishment, playfulness, balance or tranquillity is a wonderful opportunity for embracing magical moments. We need only open our eyes, arms and hearts to experience more of these moments. Though some may last but a short time, they can bring pure joy and enchantment. I call such magical moments: highlights.

Let me give you a personal example. I used to dread taking long car journeys due to my dislike of sitting in traffic jams. Now, it seems virtually impossible to travel anywhere by car without getting stuck in a traffic jam. Knowing this, at the start of any long journey I'll call into a service station and buy myself a treat. In my case it is usually a comedy CD. The deal is that I'm not allowed the treat until I get into a traffic jam. Now because I'm desperate to listen to my new CD, I sometimes find myself praying for a jam. I adapted this idea from the golfer Gary Player, who changed his own approach to traffic jams by viewing them as highlights, as they offered opportunities to practise slowing down and being patient because he knew that this was the key to his golfing success.

I coach people to be on the lookout for highlight opportunities. When you're feeling overwhelmed and exhausted due to the relentless pressure of change it's crucial that you seek out opportunities to experience highlights. In fact, you should actively set yourself highlight goals, such as experiencing two different highlights a day for the next week.

There is a Holocaust memorial in Boston, which has six pillars, representing the chimneys of the gas chambers in Auschwitz. Inscribed on five of the six pillars are stories which speak about the cruelty and suffering in the camps. The sixth pillar, however, represents a tale of a different sort. It tells a story about a little girl named Ilse, a childhood friend of Holocaust survivor and writer Guerda Weissman Klein. Guerda remembers that one morning, Ilse, who was about six years old, found a single raspberry somewhere in the camp. Ilse carried it all day long in a protected place in her pocket, and in the evening, her eyes shining with happiness, she presented it to her friend Guerda on a leaf. 'Imagine a world,' writes Guerda, 'in which your entire possession is one raspberry, and you still give it away to your friend.' I like this story as it captures the importance of looking for highlights even in the bleakest of circumstances.

It is possible to do this even when you feel like you don't have a minute to spare and everything seems like a real drag. Why not stop for a second and enjoy some scenery? Pause a while to listen to the sounds of nature? Spend five minutes looking out of your hotel window at the city lights? Admire the view as your aeroplane lands? Take the time to listen to your favourite piece of music whilst not doing anything else at the same time? Slow down and savour the taste of your lunch without checking phone or email messages? The opportunities to enjoy a moment are out there, but only if you look for them.

Here are ten ideas to get you started:

1. On your way to work next week make the effort to enjoy the route. You'll be amazed at what you see.
2. Deliberately read a favourite magazine or newspaper, listen to a new radio station or watch a TV programme you really enjoy.
3. Plan a monthly lunch with a friend.

4. Get out of your normal environment for at least half a day a week. At least 70 per cent of what you think about is contained in your immediate environment.

5. Ask your kids to help you solve a problem you're working on.

6. Allocate twice as much time as you normally would to solving a problem and enjoy the lack of pressure.

7. Take a walk in the park during your lunch break.

8. Listen to the music charts. Do you know what's number one at the moment?

9. Read a book for pleasure.

10. Watch a TV programme or film that makes you laugh.

If you are going to start spotting opportunities to enjoy highlights, you must avoid being mentally elsewhere. Remember the point in the previous chapter about the direction of your focus? Although you are physically present in a highlight situation you are not able to really enjoy the moment because your mind is preoccupied by something else.

Imagine reading a bedtime story to your child but spending all of the time thinking about other things. Or being on a country walk but mentally being back in the office and planning the next day's meeting. These are perfect opportunities to embrace a highlight but you are mentally in the wrong place. Dealing with change requires you to be good at being in the moment, not only when you are carrying out a task but also when you are switched off and relaxing. You must really be able to connect with the magic in a highlight moment and use the experience to refresh yourself and recharge your batteries.

There are always opportunities to enjoy highlights if you look closely. If you genuinely cannot find the time each day to spend just a handful of minutes embracing highlights in this way then you will struggle to cope with the demands that change forces upon you. If you need some extra incentive to find the time, it is worth bearing in mind that on average, parents spend less than thirty minutes a week effectively communicating with their children yet spend over three hours a night watching television.

Highlights are the very things that can help us navigate our way through challenging times. Professor Orlick claims that this approach is an essential part of reducing stress, staying healthy and enjoying life. Fundamentally, it's about controlling your thinking. There's only one person in control of your thoughts and that's you. Although you can't always control the circumstances, you can control your reaction to them and how you go about maintaining a positive outlook. Focusing on and embracing highlights helps us to do this.

Make a list of highlights you will enjoy in the next month.

Perspective

Gordon Strachan played for Ferguson at Aberdeen and Manchester United. He was offered a telling insight into the level of commitment which football management requires and the toll it takes on our ability to maintain perspective.

'I was given a poignant insight into this,' he says, 'when Alex's wife, Cathy, who had been experiencing a number of health problems, was rushed into hospital. It was a very traumatic time for Fergie, and because of our long association with him, from our Aberdeen days, my wife Lesley was more than willing to help him out by doing some of his ironing and shopping and looking after his sons, Mark, Jason and Darren. That was the closest I have ever got to him, and my most vivid memory of our relationship is of him sitting in our front room and pouring his heart out over his perception of the way he had treated his family.

'Cathy's illness provoked Fergie to show a side of himself that I had never seen before. While talking about not having given her and his children enough attention, he became so emotional that he burst into tears, the very last thing you would have expected of someone with his image.'

'I did not see my sons grow up, but I saw an entire generation of young players grow up,' Ferguson once offered regretfully. Strachan notes that when he made his own transition to management, 'That memory helped shape my own outlook, attitude and approach to the job.'

Learning to switch our perspective, understanding what is important, is critical to managing our outlook on change. Studies carried out by creativity expert Edward de Bono have shown that 90 per cent of our errors in thinking are due to our perception. A disturbing example of how our perspective can affect our judgement came in a survey by one of America's leading medical experts, Dr Robert Goldman, before the 2000 Sydney Olympic Games. Dr Goldman asked 200 world-class athletes the following far-reaching question: if a pill existed that would make you unbeatable for the next five years, after which you would die – would you take it? Incredibly, 52 per cent responded in the affirmative. It is also worth noting that the Sydney Games recorded the highest number of athletes failing drug tests.

This lesson of allowing ourselves some perspective is behind one of the world's most popular love songs.

Something in the way she moves,
Reminds me of ... a cauliflower.

These lyrics from the famous Beatles song 'Something' are not the ones you may remember, but they were the original ones. George Martin, the legendary producer, said that when George Harrison first started to write, he would agonise for hours over a single word. John Lennon understood the importance of perspective and suggested a simple solution. 'Just put in a word,' John said. 'Any word. Just make sure that it scans, carry on with the next line and then come back to it later when you have got some perspective.'

Harrison had the first line: *Something in the way she moves*. He also had the start of the second line: *Reminds me of* – . He wanted five syllables but nothing worked. Lennon completed the line for him: *Reminds me of – a cauliflower*. 'Now get on with it,' he said. George could continue writing his song, even if it would take him a little more time – and perspective – to eventually find the words to replace Lennon's favourite vegetable. Eventually, *a cauliflower* was replaced by *no other lover*.

When you are going through a particularly difficult phase it is natural to get bogged down by immediate demands and challenges. When the pressure of change is building and you just can't see any light at the end of the tunnel, it's critical that you somehow keep a balanced perspective. This is more than just establishing a work-life balance – it's about constantly keeping clear in your mind what the important things are.

Bill Gates understands the importance of perspective, which helped him become the richest man in the world, then give away most of that wealth to the charitable foundation he runs with his wife.

Twice a year, he goes away by himself to a remote cabin, armed with a stack of ideas from his Microsoft team, and reads, reflects and thinks big thoughts away from the daily grind. Among the business ideas to receive the green light from the boss after these retreats have been Microsoft's Web browser and its online videogame business. Google has also brought this approach into the working lives of its staff, who are given 10 per cent of their time to dream up new ideas they are passionate about. One idea which has emerged from this approach has been Google News – a news service that ranks stories from the world's media and organises this information for the user.

Psychologists describe this approach as the bath, the bed and the bus syndrome. It's named after, in reverse order, the occasions when Einstein suddenly understood, whilst sitting on a tram in Zurich, how the perception of time and space is affected by the relative motion of the observer; when Mozart heard the whole of a symphony in his head at one moment whilst lying in bed; and when Archimedes, upon realising his principle of water displacement, leapt from his bath and ran through Syracuse shouting 'Eureka!' The message is really quite straightforward. When change is dispiriting, when one difficulty after another seems to come upon you, when the pressure seems relentless and never ending, when no one appreciates all the hard work you are putting in, it is crucial to keep a healthy sense of perspective.

Ferguson learned this lesson following the advice of his chairman, Martin Edwards, who suggested that unless he found a hobby or distraction to offer him a sense of perspective, his unhealthy workload might kill him. 'The football-watching public probably saw me as an obsessive who seldom looked beyond Manchester United for entertainment. It was an accurate perception,' he admits. He took a rare day off and went with his wife to the spiritual home of jump racing, Cheltenham. He quickly became hooked. He recalls: 'Inevitably I found myself saying to Cathy in the aftermath "Do you fancy buying a horse? I think it will be a release for me." "Where did you get that one from?" she said. "Alex – the problem is that you will want to buy every bloody horse."'

He bought his first racehorse in 1996: Queensland Star, named after a ship his father had helped build. 'It opened a release valve for me. Instead of stagnating in my office or burning time in endless telephone conversations, I could switch my thoughts to the turf. It was a welcome distraction from the gruelling business of football – and that's why I threw myself into it, to enable me to escape the obsession with my job.'

Brian Clough regularly spoke of the importance of putting the game in a wider context. In the early 1980s, when he was leading Nottingham Forest to unprecedented heights of success, he took his players to the local coalfields to show them what he felt 'real work' was like and to remind them just how lucky they were to be professional footballers. On another occasion, he postponed training to take his team to a high security prison to reinforce their sense of good fortune.

Ferguson had his own reminder of this through his friendship with Jock Stein. 'I remember Stein telling me of his experiences working in the mines. He said: "You go down that pit shaft, a mile underground. You can't see a thing. The guy next to you, you don't know who he is. And yet he is the best friend you will ever have."' Ferguson paused. 'All of these lessons congeal in your character. And they never leave you.'

Ferguson's sense of perspective remained an important aspect of his ability to deal with pressure. Despite his vow to, as he later put it, 'knock Liverpool off their fucking perch', he was the first public figure from outside Liverpool to visit the Merseyside club's Anfield stadium after the Hillsborough disaster, to show his grief and support. Without the media ever getting wind of it, he presented a substantial cheque to the disaster fund.

It was the same with journalists. Although he treated the media with barely disguised contempt, when David Meek, the former *Manchester Evening News* correspondent, was diagnosed with cancer, he was able to appreciate the human impact. 'I had to break the news to Alex that I would be unable to ghost-write his programme notes for the first time in sixteen years,' Meek recalls. 'He wanted to know why and when I told him I was going into hospital for an operation he looked me in the eye and said exactly what I wanted to hear: "You can handle it."

'There was a huge bouquet waiting for me at the hospital. Then I was convalescing at home a week later and, out of the blue, the phone rang. There was no introduction. He didn't even say who it was. A voice just growled down the line: "The Scottish beast is on its way!" He was at my front door twenty minutes later and the point is he didn't have to do that. He's an extremely busy man. We had a pleasant afternoon, chatting about football and families. I'll never forget how kind and supportive he was.'

As an exercise in testing your own ability to maintain appropriate perspective, consider what your personal triggers are for losing it. Ferguson's trigger was a photograph which he referred to as 'Dante's Inferno', pinned up in the dressing room. It showed him and the players sitting on the United bench, faces distraught as they learned they had lost the League title in 1992. 'It was a reminder to make sure it never happened again,' he explains.

Becoming aware of these triggers is the first step to doing something about them. What are the types of things that lead you to relinquish your grasp on a balanced way of thinking about the stresses you are experiencing? Make a list of them on a piece of paper.

Your triggers may be related to your working hours, the mounting pressure you are experiencing, the attitude of your boss, the challenge of getting your work-life balance right. They will be different for all of us but you need to know what yours are.

When you are aware of your triggers, you can devise a plan for managing your outlook. This plan can have two parts. First, what are the special things in your life that you should focus on and appreciate? What are the things which remind you of how fortunate you are? Secondly, what experiences could you give yourself to help you put things into perspective? In other words, what's your equivalent of the footballers visiting a coal mine? You might want to consider the following:

What do you appreciate most?
What do you most enjoy doing?
When are you at your happiest?
Write down the answers.

To finish this chapter, I want to remind you that your outlook is your own to control. Think about how you manage it and consider the positive impact some slight modifications might have. Imagine how much better you would perform if you had an optimistic outlook, made the most of embracing highlights and kept a balanced perspective at all times. Such an approach will help you cope with any kind of change.

Change the Record

Listening Poem

His thoughts were slow,
His words were few
And never made to glisten.
But he was a joy
Wherever he went
You should have heard him listen.

Anon

Be hungry for feedback

As an avid quiz competitor, Sir Alex Ferguson has twice accepted the challenge to win one million pounds for charity by sitting in the chair to answer questions on the popular television programme *Who Wants to be a Millionaire?* On each occasion, he has reached the £32,000 question before bowing out. Despite his assertion that he is 'never afraid to make a decision and then never look back', he has shown a remarkable willingness to seek feedback and learn from others before he does so. On the quiz show, he has done this through astute use of his lifeline, which enables him to ask the audience for help. We will see how he has used a similar tactic in his professional life, with more successful results. One approach to developing your ability to lead change is to actively look for feedback. But it will not find you. You have to ask.

Top performers, whether in sport or business, are generally very keen to receive feedback because they know how important it is to keep adapting and improving. You need to be very aware of your strengths and your areas for potential development. Feedback is a crucial way of acquiring this information, but it can be tough because you may not always like what you hear.

In a discussion about feedback, it seems apt that Ferguson enjoys telling a story about Jimi Hendrix, who had a humble approach to fuel his desire to become a legendary rock guitarist. His manager claims that he once spent a whole night in a club listening to a musician who was charitably referred to as 'the worst guitar player in the history of the planet Earth'. When his manager asked why he wanted to stay to listen to the noise, Hendrix coolly replied, 'So far, this is bad, but he might just play something that has never been played before. If he does – I want to be here to learn from it.'

Although you may not always like the feedback you get, you should be able to learn something useful from it. Adopting such an approach is a characteristic of someone who will successfully survive change.

Let's play a quick game to illustrate how Ferguson applied this lesson.

Question:
Steve Bruce
Eric Cantona
Cristiano Ronaldo
What do the signings of all three players have in common?

Answer:
They were all signed because of Ferguson's willingness to seek feedback.

Example 1: Steve Bruce

Bryan Robson recalls a difficult period towards the end of the 1980s when injuries to the United team's defenders had an adverse effect on results. 'We had problems with injuries in the middle of the defence and I knew the boss had decided he needed to bring in another centre half. I like to think I helped him find his man.

'I used to go through the players' ratings in *The People* newspaper and keep a close eye on those who consistently received high marks. I said to the gaffer, "That lad at Norwich, Bruce, always seems to get star rating. Has anyone looked at him?"' Robson's question prompted Ferguson to take a formal interest in the player and soon afterwards, he went on to sign him for a bargain £825,000. Ferguson subsequently described Bruce as 'central to creating the club culture' for the next eight years.

Example 2: Eric Cantona

Steve Bruce reciprocated the approach when Ferguson chose to consult him and his defensive partner Gary Pallister about the merits of a certain player. Pallister recalls a conversation they had with Ferguson at the back of the team coach: 'One night he asked Steve and myself what we thought of Eric Cantona, who was playing for Leeds United. Our answer: "Yes, he's a player, he's got something, and he's got something different."' That 'something different' was the confidence, assurance and swagger Cantona brought to help the club and Ferguson win their first League title. 'He was the tin opener, the one who could create chances others couldn't see,' was Ferguson's assessment of the French legend.

Example 3: Cristiano Ronaldo

In the summer of 2003, Manchester United played against Sporting Lisbon in a pre-season friendly. Irish full back John O'Shea was pitted against a young eighteen-year-old winger. 'After the first pass, I was prompted to howl: "For Christ's sake John, get tight to him!"' Ferguson recalls. O'Shea could merely shrug his shoulders. 'A look of pain and bewilderment was creeping across his face,' Ferguson says. 'The other players sat with me in the dugout were saying, "Bloody hell, boss, he's some player, him."' According to Rio Ferdinand, 'We could all see that this tall skinny kid was amazing, I wasn't the only one saying we should sign him.' Ferguson assured them that he would. He declared, 'We're not leaving this ground until we've got that boy signed.' Within hours of the game's final whistle, Cristiano Ronaldo was a Manchester United player.

So who do you get feedback from?

A recent study, which compared forty-one Nobel laureates in the sciences with a sample of their similarly experienced peers, found that a major difference between the two groups was that the Nobel laureates canvassed a wider range of opinions than the other scientists. They were open to a variety of opinions.

Why? Well, you may have heard of a syndrome known as Fundamental Attribution Error (FAE), to which we are all susceptible. This means that we tend to look for feedback from people with similar outlooks to ourselves. My favourite experiment investigating how FAE works was a study of how Europeans honked their car horns.

The experiment was incredibly simple. A man and woman drove around Germany, France, Spain and Italy in a grey VW Beetle with Australian insignia to distinguish the driver's nationality. When they drove through a town, they would sit in front of traffic lights and when the lights turned green, they didn't move. The experimenters then noted how long it took for the drivers behind to begin honking their horns.

The Italians proved the most impatient, honking their horns on average after about five seconds. Next were the Spanish, at about the six-second mark. The French came in at about seven seconds and the Germans proved most patient at about seven and a half seconds.

In the second stage of the experiment, the Australian insignia was swapped for German and the same behaviour of stopping at traffic lights was repeated. This time, the Italians, Spanish and French all honked their horns much more quickly (between three and four seconds). In Germany, however, the situation was quite different. Because they believed the driver of the Beetle was a fellow German, the drivers behind were immediately more sympathetic. Once again, they allowed the vehicle the longest amount of time before sounding their horns, but this time the wait was even longer, at eight seconds. Something as simple as an insignia had affected the drivers' feelings of similarity (or dissimilarity) and had a significant impact on their patience and thus on the time that passed before they began sounding their horns.

In other words, one of the real dangers of not gathering a wide range of feedback is that small groups of similar minds can easily only tell you what they think you want to hear. The extreme version of this is the kind of groupthink that happened in the planning of the US Bay of Pigs invasion of Cuba, where the members of President John F. Kennedy's advisory group bonded so well that the possibility of dissent seemed practically unthinkable.

'I read a lot of history,' Sir Alex Ferguson admits. 'And in most history books, there won't be a mention of sport, but there are always insights you can learn.' One particular example was Doris Kearns Goodwin's political biography of Abraham Lincoln, *Team of Rivals*, which his friend Alastair Campbell had presented to him. 'I couldn't get enough of it,' Ferguson says. 'What was fascinating was how he held together all these big personalities, the ones who had tried to stop him becoming President, to make sure they stayed roughly on the same track.' The parallels with his world were obvious. 'I can learn about the art of team building and team management from this,' he thought. 'It's all about managing people and relationships, in the end.'

This management of his support staff was an important feature of Ferguson's tenure at United. 'Manchester United have not played in the same style for these 25 years; we have bought new players to adapt to new systems, sometimes to pull further away from our counterparts and sometimes to narrow a gap,' Ferguson said. Shuffling his backroom team allowed him to see challenges through a fresh pair of eyes and prevented players from going stale on the training ground.

When he arrived at Old Trafford, he was accompanied by Archie Knox, a trusted colleague who had been his right-hand man when Aberdeen were top of the League in Scotland in 1980, and they were together for the club's finest ever hour – the 1983 triumph against the mighty Real Madrid in the European Cup Winners' Cup final. Knox remained with Ferguson throughout his painful early years before his departure to Glasgow Rangers in 1991. He was replaced by former United favourite Brian Kidd, who had been the club's youth development officer during a period when the famous 'Class of '92' were being nurtured behind the scenes, and they were side by side as the club ended its 26-year title drought.

Kidd, in turn, was Ferguson's longest serving assistant manager, a position he held for seven years until he was enticed away by Blackburn Rovers, who wanted him as their new manager. During their seven years together the Ferguson/Kidd partnership garnered four League titles and two doubles.

It was the introduction of the largely unknown Steve McClaren as Kidd's successor that was arguably the most inspired. After the disappointment of losing Kidd, Ferguson said he instructed his staff to scour the land 'for the best (and hardest working) coach out there'. Future England manager McClaren, who was assistant to Jim Smith at Derby County, joined the club early in 1999, just months before the most glorious chapter in United's history – the treble. Ferguson has since said of McClaren, 'He was organised, strong and always looking for new ideas, Steve was made for management. He was effervescent, energetic with a good personality.' When McClaren left after two and a half success-laden years, Ferguson drafted in former South Africa boss Carlos Queiroz as his deputy. He has described the Portuguese coach as 'just brilliant', and has credited him with introducing new ideas to the club. Ferguson says, 'He was the closest you could be to being Manchester United manager without actually holding the title. He took responsibility for a lot of issues he did not have to get involved in.'

When Queiroz left, Ferguson chose ex-Rangers and Everton boss Walter Smith as his assistant before the latter was appointed manager of the Scottish national side. Ferguson then induced Queiroz to return for the next four years, in the course of which United won two League titles and the Champions League in 2008. On his appointment as manager of Portugal, Queiroz was replaced by former United midfielder Mike Phelan, who stayed with Ferguson during his final five seasons at Old Trafford, a period which saw United lift three more League titles.

During his time in the dugout, Ferguson would also continue to take plenty of advice from his mentors. He recalls the value of listening to Jock Stein – the first man to take a British club to the summit of European football, when he guided Glasgow Celtic to an unlikely European Cup triumph in 1967 – before Aberdeen's historic 2–1 victory in the 1983 European Cup Winners' Cup final against Real Madrid. Ferguson invited Stein to his pre-final training camp, where he received some advice about how he should handle the opposition's manager, Alfredo Di Stefano, regarded as one of the game's greatest ever players.

Ferguson said, 'One interesting suggestion he made was that I should buy the great Di Stefano a gift of good whisky. "Let him feel important," said Jock, "as if you are thrilled just to be in the final, making up the numbers."' Ferguson recalls how 'Di Stefano was certainly taken aback when I presented him with the whisky on the eve of the match.' The advice came in useful again eight years later when Ferguson presented his opposite number, Johan Cruyff, with a bottle of whisky before United and Barcelona went head to head in the final of the same competition. United beat Barcelona, again 2–1, on a thrilling night in Rotterdam.

Who might you ask for feedback? Pick people who you respect and who will give you honest and practical views. And what you ask may well be different for each individual. Some questions could include: What is the first thing you think of when you think of me?

What one word or phrase sums up my personality? What one thing could I change for my own benefit? What do you value most about me? What do you think are my greatest talents, strengths or skills?

You might find it useful to organise your answers in three columns, as in the table below:

WHO	WHEN and HOW	ON WHAT
Three people whose views I respect, and who I could ask for feedback.	*When is the best time to ask for their help and what format should they use when giving feedback – written or verbal?*	*Specifically, what shall I ask each for feedback on?*
1.		
2.		
3.		

Managing your reaction to feedback: Remember the 3.5 minute rule!

So, you have decided to take me up on my suggestion to get feedback. What now? Well, your reaction is important.

In America, analysis of medical malpractice lawsuits against doctors show that there are many highly skilled doctors who get sued a lot and there are also many doctors who make lots of mistakes and yet never face legal action. The main difference between the two types of doctor is just 3.5 minutes. It works like this.

The doctors who are never sued spend an average of just 3.5 minutes longer with each patient than the ones who do tend to get sued (18.5 minutes versus 15 minutes in appointment times). Interestingly, there is no real difference in the quality of the advice which the two types of doctor give to their patients. The real difference appears to be how well they listen.

We are all capable of listening to about 600 words a minute, yet are only able to speak a maximum of 150 words in the same time. In effect, we can listen four times faster than anyone can talk. This means that when we get feedback, we tend to react quickly to the first things we hear. Instead of talking, we should stop and listen. This was a lesson which some of Sir Alex Ferguson's players had to learn the hard way. Perhaps the most significant example was Peter Schmeichel, the giant Danish goalkeeper, who played his part in an argument which some witnesses suggest was the most explosive of Ferguson's career.

In January 1994, United were holed up in the away dressing room at Anfield, home to United's fiercest rivals Liverpool, when an angry Ferguson launched a broadside at his 'keeper after his team had let a 3–0 lead slip to draw 3–3 in a match which is still regarded as one of the Premier League's greatest games. Ferguson cared little for the view of the neutral. According to both Schmeichel and his team-mate Gary Pallister, United's greatest ever stopper had incurred his manager's wrath for the offence of what Ferguson perceived to be repeatedly taking poor goal kicks. Schmeichel said, 'I was speechless, I felt he was blaming the result on me, and it seemed – although it was probably a bit of an exaggeration – that in the second half I had been forced to take a goal kick about once every twenty seconds.'

In hindsight, Schmeichel now surmises that his boss's rant had less to do with poor goal kicks, an accusation the 'keeper still refutes, and more to do with the frustration at watching his side throw away a three-goal lead at Liverpool of all places, a humiliation he could not accept. Schmeichel says: 'I was already angry at myself! How can a good football team throw away a 3–0 lead and not be able to do a single thing about it? That was the question I was asking myself when Ferguson started to attack me.

'At this point I lost control of myself, and I would imagine that in a calmer and more reasonable light of reflection he would agree with me that neither of us truly meant what followed: a gigantic argument which with the speed of lightning reached such a personal level that I don't care to mention what was said. That's how embarrassing it was. It turned into a battle between two will-powers, neither of which was interested or capable of backing down.

'I said the most awful things. I questioned his capabilities as a manager. I aired doubts about his personal qualities.'

Steve Bruce, watching in stunned silence, recalled, 'Ferguson didn't keep anything back either and at one point he threatened to throw a cup of tea in Schmeichel's face.' The goalkeeper ended the row when 'I just turned my back on him and headed for the showers, embarrassingly aware of the fact that it had grown deadly silent in the changing room.' In a meeting which took place two days after the confrontation, Ferguson invited Schmeichel in. 'He asked me to sit down, looked at me for a while and said: "I suppose you realise that I have no choice but to give you the sack?"'

Schmeichel offered Ferguson an unconditional apology, which was accepted. But, Ferguson said, 'I would still not change my decision.' What did alter his thinking, however, was when he heard his goalkeeper apologise to his team-mates for his 'childish' behaviour. Ferguson was impressed by the sincerity of Schmeichel's actions and enjoyed another five and a half years of loyal service from the Dane.

Clearly, if you have followed the advice and chosen a wide range of people from whom to get feedback, not everything you receive may be positive. You are likely to receive some feedback that you either don't like or don't agree with. Managing your reaction to this is also part of surviving change. Let me detail the six stages we go through when we receive feedback. They are:

SHOCK
ANGER
DENIAL
RATIONALISATION
ACCEPTANCE
ACTION

When I teach these six stages of reaction, I colour code the six letters. *Shock*, *anger* and *denial* are all part of the emotional response, which is quite often strong and negative – for this reason it is in what I call the red zone. *Rationalisation* and *acceptance* are thinking-related and are about coming to terms with the feedback in a constructive and considered manner. I call this the blue zone, due to it being more mellow and calm.

Finally, the green zone is about moving on and taking *action* and changing our behaviours. Having understood and appreciated the feedback and its value, you are now ready to implement plans to change your approach.

Make a chart of the six stages like the one below and fill in your own typical responses.

The red zone: emotions	SHOCK	*Wow — I didn't expect that. I'm really surprised by those comments.*	
	ANGER	*How dare they say that! Wait until I get the chance to get my own back.*	
	DENIAL	*I'm not like that at all. I never behave like that. I can't understand why they would pick that one example out.*	
The blue zone: thinking	RATIONALI-SATION	*Yes, but the reason they think that is because they don't know what kind of pressure I am under. Anyway, that's the way I am and why should I change? Look at my overall performance. I'm delivering the goods, aren't I?*	
	ACCEPTANCE	*OK, I accept that I need to change.*	
The green zone: behaviour	ACTION	*Right, what is my action plan? I am seriously committed to developing my performance by using this feedback in the most practical way I can. I shall start tomorrow.*	

Those who manage change well get through these six phases as quickly as they can. They don't dwell too long on the early stages of shock, anger, denial and rationalisation. They quickly move towards accepting the feedback and decide how it can help them. The ability to navigate his way through the six stages was a common feature of Ferguson's management. 'You could have a furious argument with him and the next day, he would behave completely normal with you again,' says Lee Sharpe. 'It was as if he had forgotten it and moved on.'

That is precisely what Ferguson did in 1991 following a row with Gary Pallister. The argument happened in the dressing room at half-time during an FA Cup clash with Queens Park Rangers. Ferguson accused Pallister of being bullied by an opposing striker. When Pallister disagreed, Ferguson retorted by calling the central defender a 'wimp'. The insult was 'like throwing a match into a barrel of gunpowder' according to Pallister, who describes the stand-up argument which ensued as 'torrid'. He says, 'I don't have the slightest doubt that, fleetingly at least, Ferguson was bent on lamping me.'

Following the intervention of backroom staff the pair were separated, but Ferguson told Pallister he would not be playing the second half and they continued to 'hurl some terrible words at each other'. Ferguson was persuaded to reconsider his decision by his assistant, Archie Knox, who then attempted to persuade Pallister to go back onto the pitch for the second half. 'Do it for your team-mates and prove him wrong,' Knox told the fuming Pallister, who agreed and helped the team win 2–1.

The next day, Pallister arrived for training and was braced for another confrontation. He was shocked by the reception he received. He says: 'Ferguson sat down, gazed at me across his desk and dropped the biggest bombshell I could have imagined. I can recall his exact words: "I want to apologise for what I said at half-time in the game."

'I sat there, utterly flummoxed, no doubt with my jaw sagging. You could have flattened me with the proverbial feather!'

Ferguson continued: 'I went too far. I said things that I should never have said. It was wrong.' He then explained to Pallister that he would not countenance having rows with his players during the interval. He said: 'I've got ten minutes to get my message across, as quickly, clearly and maybe bluntly as possible but I can accept when I get it wrong.'

One final tip on the feedback process is to ensure that you get feedback on your strengths as well as your development needs. It is really important that you learn to maximise your strengths as well as managing your weaknesses, so make sure that you devote quality time to assessing the extent to which you are doing this.

Change Your Confidence Levels

Flatter me, and I may not believe you.
Criticise me, and I may not like you.
Ignore me, and I may not forgive you.
Encourage me, and I will not forget you.

William Arthur Ward

Sir Alex Ferguson recalls the winter of 2005 with all the affection reserved for appendicitis: early elimination from the Champions League, the abuse he suffered from his own fans during a defeat to Blackburn Rovers, humiliation in drawing with non-league Burton Albion in the FA Cup, the breakdown of his relationship with Roy Keane and the skipper's subsequent dismissal, the near incessant speculation about his future, and the eroding of the bond with his star striker Ruud Van Nistelrooy, resulting in the player's departure. 'This was supposed to be the autumn of Ferguson's career but it felt more like its winter, harsh and unforgiving,' Daniel Taylor wrote in the *Guardian*. 'It was the season when his own fans called for him to be sacked, the press parked their tanks on his lawn and his relationship with the media hit an all-time low. It was the third year since they could call themselves champions. It was the season of Chelsea, led by Jose Mourinho.'

The press found Ferguson in his most combative, fight-the-world mode. They were continually braced for the Ferguson who didn't suffer fools. The Ferguson who responded to a *Daily Telegraph* reporter's innocent question, after one trophy-less season, 'Where did it go wrong?' with the withering retort, 'That's a good question. But it would take a whole interview to get it and that's an interview you're never going to fucking get.' In *The Times*, Simon Barnes wrote that Ferguson was 'a sad self-caricature' and 'a failure [who] got where he wanted to be but didn't stay there'. Ferguson, he declared, 'should have gone 18 months ago. Staying on was the wrong decision for the team and for himself.' Even Ferguson's great friend, Hugh McIlvanney, the journalist who helped him write his first autobiography, *Managing My Life*, suggested that retirement was imminent. He wrote the following words of advice in *The Sunday Times*: 'He must never run the risk of being dispatched … Eventually, there comes a moment when the best and bravest of fighters shouldn't answer the bell. That moment may be upon us.'

Despite the swirling winds of discontent that swept around him, Ferguson's demeanour within the club was never less than sunny. One morning, Daniel Taylor witnessed him coming down the stairs at the training ground, singing an old Josef Locke song to Kath, the receptionist:

Hear my song Violetta
Hear my song beneath the moon
Come to me, in my gondola
Waiting on the old lagoon

Fellow journalist David Meek, who covered Manchester United for thirty-seven years, nodded knowingly upon learning of this. 'He's always sunny, regardless of results,' said Meek. 'He's especially at his best when there's a problem, when he's backed into a corner and needs to come out fighting. He shows supreme self-confidence and that attitude is reflected by his players and gets United out of scrapes.'

In his autobiography, Ferguson wrote: 'I work hard at making sure my worries do not manifest themselves in the dressing room and I felt my demeanour was good.' He did this because 'Belief and confidence are very important, and instilling the right outlook is my priority.' Ferguson stressed, 'It's not something that can be built overnight but that is what I work towards and I love every minute of it.'

Former Manchester United striker Mark Hughes recalls that when he was at the club, the United players would wait after a defeat for the first broken crest to appear on the back page of any newspaper. Beloved by tabloid sports editors, it is a favoured short-hand visual device to illustrate United's problems. 'Not that United merely have problems,' suggests Hughes. 'This is not a club that has defeats. It has crises.'

This shouldn't be a surprise. In the world of the newsroom, the phrases 'good news' and 'bad news' take on the opposite meanings to those they have in the real world. For a journalist, a 'good news' day is a day filled with mayhem, murder and mischief. A 'bad news' day is a day when nothing in particular happens. This is why Ferguson claimed to pay no attention to what was written in the papers: 'I have a mechanism that says, "Forget it," and I don't read the tabloids. Although my lawyers do,' he added ominously.

This negative focus is not solely confined to our emotions, either. At a deeper level we generally seem to be hard-wired to focus on the negative. A group of psychologists reviewed over two hundred newspaper articles and concluded that, for a wide range of human behaviour and perception, a general principle holds true: bad has a stronger influence than good.

Here is a little puzzle. Look at the following sentence:

OPPORTUNITYISNOWHERE

What did you see?

Opportunity is nowhere?
Opportunity is snow here?
Opportunity is now here?

If you read it as it was intended, you would have seen 'opportunity is now here'. But if you are like the vast majority of adults you probably read 'opportunity is nowhere'. What's my point? Most of us are conditioned to read with negative eyes. This is significant for a number of reasons.

Dr Shad Helmstetter, an American child psychologist, estimates that in the first sixteen years of our lives, people say no to us about 148,000 times. Get a calculator out and divide 148,000 by 16 and then by 365; it comes to 25 no's a day. He also estimates that on average, parents speak to their children in a negative manner over 90 per cent of the time. No wonder that in related tests, 90 per cent of UK children have a positive self-image at the age of four and yet this figure drops to just 5 per cent by the age of sixteen. This problem-seeking mindset is a shortcoming in each of us. Psychologists who have studied our instinctive attraction to the negative have reached some fascinating conclusions. In an exhaustive study, the English language was found to contain 558 words that describe emotions; 62 per cent of them are negative versus 28 per cent that refer to positive feelings.

It seems fairly obvious to suggest that humans are programmed to focus on failure and disappointment far more than on success and achievement. Usually, it is so automatic that we don't even notice it or the effect it has on our moods and feelings. When we are low on confidence, the voice in our head is typically negative and irrational and we find it very easy to recall all of those disastrous days in the middle of change when everything went wrong and we were left feeling embarrassed and incompetent.

Whenever we find ourselves in a similar situation, our brain quickly recalls these previous catastrophes and regenerates the same awful feelings of despair and anxiety. This type of thinking, of course, sends us off into a spiral of negativity, causing us to lose confidence about how well we can cope with change. We are then trapped in a cycle of low confidence that contributes to a poor performance, which results in further damage to our self-confidence and even more disappointing results.

Avoiding this cycle was something that Alex Ferguson would continually monitor, moving quickly to address the signs before it became an issue. Ferguson had a metaphor he used to describe why he did this: 'I tell the players that the bus is moving on. This club has to progress. And the bus won't wait for them. I tell them to get on board. Or they'll miss out. At this club we don't stop, we don't take rests, we don't feel sorry for ourselves. We go on and on.' As Gary Neville once explained, 'At the training ground he's never one to lead the sessions but somehow he never misses anything. He'll suddenly appear, walking up and down the sidelines, chatting to coaches, but always alert. There's nothing that his eyes and ears don't pick up.'

Managing your relationships with the significant people in your life is hugely important in helping you to maintain a positive attitude towards change. The approach adopted by Ferguson and his coaches is supported in a study carried out in the early 1980s by psychologist John Gottman, who researched why some married couples stay together whilst others break up. Professor Gottman watched a series of couples closely as they went about their daily interactions and found that the answer he was looking for lay in the tiny details of those apparently inconsequential everyday exchanges. Banal as they seemed on the surface, at another level they were highly nuanced emotional exchanges. Psychologists suggest that during the conversations we have with others, we make signals or 'bids'. A bid is something that invites a response.

Often, we don't notice how we are responding – until it is too late and the damage has been done. The good news is that these bids are very easy to spot and pretty easy to change if we know where to look and are willing to make the effort. The impact of Gottman's work was enormous. Based on his insights a whole new approach to marriage counselling was developed. So how does this work, and how did Ferguson use the principles in relation to creating change?

Picture the scene. You see one of your players make a silly mistake, which costs the team a goal. The player acknowledges the mistake. At this moment, Ferguson would watch the reaction of the other players to their struggling team-mate. They now have the chance to respond in one of three ways:

1. *They could acknowledge the mistake and reply to it in a positive way*: 'Come on. You're better than that.' Or 'Don't worry. Let's put it right.' In psychologist-speak, this is called a 'turning towards response' or a 'response bid'.
2. *They could acknowledge it in a negative way*: 'You are useless. What are you doing?' or, 'How can you be so stupid?' Unsurprisingly, this is called an 'against bid'.
3. *Or they could just stay silent*: '!' This is called an 'away from' bid. They don't engage with what you've done. In effect they ignore your bid.

Whatever response they choose will determine what you do next. But only the first one is likely to encourage you to make another attempt. Faced with an 'against' or 'away from' response we are more likely to make an unconscious mental note not to bother next time. The research shows that, when we use plenty of 'turning towards' bids, the effects are enormous. Couples where the exchanges are predominantly 'towards' stay together. In fact, there is even a magic ratio. If we manage a ratio of 5:1 positive ('towards') responses to negative ('away from or against') responses, we are likely to have a healthy, long-lasting partnership.

This ratio is also important both in sports teams and in the workplace. In a recent survey, 99 out of 100 people reported that they wanted to be around positive people and nine out of ten reported being more productive when they were around positive people. This is supported by another recent study which found that workplaces with positive-to-negative ratios greater than 3:1 are significantly more productive than teams that don't reach this ratio.

Ferguson and the assistant coaches carried this principle into training sessions and the dressing room. They would only emphasise positives in what they saw: 'There is no room for criticism on the training field,' he said. 'For a player – and for any human being – there is nothing better than hearing, "Well done."

Those are the two best words ever invented in sports. You don't need to use superlatives.'

Failing to do this makes it easy to become dragged into the pessimism cycle, something which the Australian cricket team perfected as an art form which they called 'sledging'. Former captain Mark Waugh speaks with pride about achieving the 'mental disintegration of opponents' before a ball was even bowled by reminding them verbally and in graphic detail of all their previous failures, weaknesses and mistakes. They knew that this didn't help them deliver their best.

Many commentators suggest that Alex Ferguson was not averse to employing this tactic to unsettle his rivals, a suggestion that he partially refutes. 'I did not set out to master the dark arts. It was more important to concentrate on ourselves but I did try the odd trick.' Some examples of this include his annual declaration that Manchester United were always stronger in the second half of a season. 'I did it every year. "Wait until the second half of the season," I would say. And it always worked. It crept into the minds of our players and became a nagging fear for the opposition. Second half of the season, United would come like an invasion force, with hellfire in their eyes. It became a self-fulfilling prophecy.' Ferguson stopped using this line when then Chelsea manager Carlo Ancelotti challenged its veracity. 'Alex is saying United are stronger in the second half of the season, but we are, too,' he claimed.

Perhaps the most notorious example of Ferguson's psychological 'sledges' was the concept known as 'Fergie time' – the well-established idea among football fans that an extra helping of added time would be given when Manchester United were losing. The phenomenon of Fergie time originated in 1993. United were playing Sheffield Wednesday, who were leading 1–0 after ninety minutes. The referee gave seven minutes of added time, during which Steve Bruce scored twice, clearing the way for United's first top-flight title in twenty-six years. 'Ever since then, every time United have been given quite a bit of injury time, it's been flagged up in people's heads and they've said, "Oh, United have got more Fergie time again,"' says Duncan Alexander of Opta Sports, which collates data from the games. Ferguson would symbolise the concept by standing on the touchline and tapping his watch. However, he confesses, 'I didn't keep track of the time in games. It became too hard to work out how long might be added for a stoppage to have an accurate sense of when the game should end.' He did it because of the psychological impact it carried.

'Here's the key: it was the effect it had on the other team, not ours, that counted. Seeing me tap my watch and gesticulate, the opposition would be spooked. They would immediately think another ten minutes were going to be added. Everyone knew that United had a knack of scoring late goals. Seeing me point to my timepiece, our opponents would feel they would have to defend against us through a spell of time that would feel, to them, like an eternity. They would feel besieged. They knew we never gave up and they knew we specialised in late drama.'

Yet, how often do we face change and start to 'sledge' ourselves? We must try not to fall into this cycle of despondency. Actively reconnecting your mind with some of your previous positive successes is one way to avoid it. Of course, this does not come naturally, and so we need something to help us.

There is a famous story about Pablo Picasso which illustrates how to think positively. One day Picasso welcomed a stranger into his studio. On the floor in the middle of the studio sat a large lump of rock. The visitor asked Picasso what he intended to do with it. 'From that rock, I will sculpt a lion,' he replied. The visitor was taken aback. It was hard to imagine how anyone could create anything from such a rock. In obvious awe of Picasso, he asked the master nervously what, how, where one might start the process of creating a lion from such an unpromising block of stone. 'Oh, it's very simple,' Picasso replied. 'I just take my chisel and knock off all the bits that don't look like a lion.'

This story illustrates my belief that when we need to feel confident in ourselves, it is not a process of having to invent something from nothing. Instead, it's an exercise in removing all of the bits that don't help us and keeping the bits that do.

In a survey among elite gymnasts, they were asked what they thought about during a competition. It turned out that those who were most successful – those who qualified for the Olympic team – had many of the same doubts and anxieties as their less successful team-mates. However, the difference between the two was that the Olympic qualifiers managed to combat their nerves by knocking away the bits that didn't help and keeping the encouraging parts which did. They achieved this by completing the following exercise.

The confidence peak chart

Sir Edmund Hillary, the first man to scale Mount Everest, said, 'It is not the mountain we conquer, but ourselves.' This quotation seems an appropriate way of introducing the confidence peak chart.

Take a piece of paper and draw a similar diagram. Then imagine that each of the peaks represents a significant achievement that you have accomplished. Reflect back on those achievements and record each of them in one of the mountains. Think hard about this, because it may not come easily, but I am confident that if you focus your mind, you will be able to generate at least twelve achievements of which you are genuinely proud. You can be as general as you want and relate it

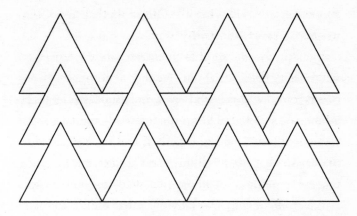

right back to your school days (riding a bicycle and learning to swim are two skills which are always worth an honourable mention). Alternatively, you could use the chart to focus on a more specific set of achievements which are directly related to a particular challenge you are facing.

It looks simple and that's because it is. My experience of using it has been positive. It presents the evidence of how you have already climbed many mountains in your life. The thing that they have in common is they are all successful achievements. You'll find that the more you go through life, the bigger your mountain range becomes and the platform for your self-belief establishes an increasingly firm base, giving you lots of evidence to use to boost your confidence when you really need it.

The confidence peak chart works even better when you describe the achievement and recall as much detail about the event as possible: how you were feeling, what you were thinking, how you behaved. In the chapter on visualisation, I explained how the process of 'reconnection' with an event will be much more powerful if it's remembered in all of its glorious Technicolor detail. Doing this exercise is like having your own personal confidence bank account. Every time you are able to stop and reflect upon your successes and reconnect in some way with a previous achievement, you are making a deposit into your confidence account. Over time, you will build up a healthy balance that will be really useful on the occasions when your confidence is a bit shaky and you need to make a withdrawal from the account.

Despite his assertion that 'winning a trophy doesn't really mean anything to me after it's gone. At the time it is the most treasured thing. But as soon as it's over, it's soon forgotten,' Alex Ferguson knew the important effect on confidence that a victory can have. Be it a Scottish Youth Cup final with his young Aberdeen charges or his first Champions League crown, Ferguson always made sure his players celebrated their triumphs and he would insist that images of these celebrations were prominently displayed throughout the club's training ground and stadium.

This was a painful lesson he had learned in 1983, when his Aberdeen team retained the Scottish Cup with a win over Rangers. He gave a television interview in which he poured cold water over the celebrations. Ferguson said, 'We're the luckiest team in the world. It was a disgrace of a performance. Our standards have been set long ago and we're not going to accept that from any Aberdeen team. No way should we take any glory from that.' He later acknowledged that this was a mistake and retracted his comments. When he picked up his first winner's medal as United boss, the FA Cup in 1990, he encouraged the wild on-pitch celebrations. As Daniel Taylor has observed, 'After every trophy Ferguson has won for United, at the final whistle he is on the pitch, arms raised, triumphantly punching the air. He embraces every single player, every single coach.'

'To watch him after a victorious cup final,' according to Taylor, 'is like peering through your fingers at a wedding as a tipsy uncle takes to the floor demanding more Jive Bunny or YMCA. Ferguson is certainly not one of those managers who prefers to stand to the side and let the players milk the moment. He is right in the thick of things, jubilant and euphoric.' Ferguson agrees: 'It is great to see the Manchester United players celebrate at the finish of a victory. The dressing room after a final is a fine place to be when you are a winner.'

To my mind, one of Ferguson's most important victories came in 2006 when United beat Wigan 4–0 in the final of the Carling Cup, ending a barren run of one trophy in three years. Captain Gary Neville remembers, 'It was as bleak as it got in my time at Old Trafford. There were a lot of question marks over the club. Arsenal had been through their "Invincibles" season and Roman Abramovich was pouring millions into Chelsea. United were going through a transitional stage with young players and there were periods when you definitely felt as though the club would never win the League again.'

That League Cup victory was the first senior medal won by Wayne Rooney and gave players like Louis Saha, Nemanja Vidic and Patrice Evra their first taste of success in the famous red jersey. Neville says, 'Looking back, this win, my first as captain, was a massive victory for the club. That success taught young players like Wayne Rooney, for whom it was his first trophy, what it was like to win.' Neville argues that it 'was the springboard to the most dominant period in the club's history', when United won four titles out of five and qualified for three out of four Champions League finals, winning in 2008. 'Being on the podium is a drug. Having a medal put round your neck and running round a stadium with the cup is addictive. I had the privilege to do it lots of times in my career and never got bored. People ask: "What was the best night of your life?" I've had around fourteen best nights in my life, always after winning a cup. It is those moments that draw teams closer and create the team spirit to go on and win more.'

Let's look at further methods you can use to build your confidence for those times when you most need it. These ideas should be used in conjunction with the confidence chart to help you keep strong foundations in place. Have a look at the ideas below. The trick is to find the one that suits you, as not everyone responds in the same way to a specific approach.

Self-talk

Have you ever noticed how young children tend to talk to themselves? This is an essential part of brain development. Psychologists have found that among children under ten years old, private speech can account for between 20 per cent and 60 per cent of the words uttered on any given day. Although it may not appear so, children are actually using this chatter to master new skills and learn how to control their behaviour.

The importance of private speech was first documented in Russia in the 1930s by a prominent psychologist named Lev Vygotsky. Say that a child is trying to learn a skill, like inserting a DVD into a player. He may ask his mum for help. As his mum puts the DVD into the machine, she explains what she is doing. ('First we push the open button. Then we place the DVD in the tray. Next, we close the tray.') The child records these instructions into his own private speech and will typically repeat the instructions out loud to direct himself.

As children get older and acquire more experience of these kinds of tasks, this private speech doesn't disappear; it just becomes internalised. In other words, it becomes our self-talk. For example, when the child learns how to play the DVD, she will no longer say aloud the instructions, 'Open, DVD, tray, play,' but she will still think them. Only if there is something the child doesn't understand will she continue to say that particular word out loud. For example, if she has difficulty understanding the need to press the play button, only the word 'play' is said aloud.

Controlling your own self-talk in order to boost your confidence is an important part of surviving change. In a recent US study of children up to the age of ten, those from troubled backgrounds were found to have more than 40 per cent of their self-talk still audible, whereas fewer than 7 per cent of children from more stable backgrounds spoke out loud. Why? Children who regularly have their learning positively reinforced progress much faster because their confidence grows.

During times of change, by regularly engaging in positive self-talk (using language to focus on your strengths and positive expectations) you will obviously start to feel more confident and more likely to do well. Equally, if you start asking yourself self-defeating questions such as 'Why does this always happen to me?' your brain will look for the exact answer by focusing on your weaknesses, mistakes and doubts and instantly tell you: 'Because you're an idiot!'

Ferguson changed his approach to understand and accommodate those who needed help with this. 'I was very aggressive when I first started in management. I am passionate and want to win all the time. But today I'm more mellowed and I can better handle those more fragile players now.'

One method he used was to draw on a collection of favourite team talks that touched on the theme of confidence. Some of his players knew them almost by heart. There was the one about the American billionaire Armand Hammer, who had the passion to continue to rise at six o'clock every morning to go to his office even when he was in his eighties. And there was the parable about a man who kept banging into the glass doors at a branch of Marks & Spencer. Ferguson used that to upbraid players who were having difficulty learning from their mistakes.

Sometimes, he sat his players down in the dressing room before a big game and challenged them about what they wanted out of life and football. He told them that some people were content to take their holidays in Blackpool every year, buy kiss-me-quick hats, eat ice creams and stroll on the promenade. And then there were some people who wanted to fly to the moon. 'Me,' Ferguson said, 'I want to fly to the moon.'

He had his favourite speech, however, one of which Gary Neville has said: 'Three or four times a season he'll make the same speech – and it never fails to work. "Look around this dressing room," he'll say, "Look at each other and be proud to be in this together." He'll point to an individual. "I'd want him on my team, and him, and him." By the time he is finished, you can feel the hairs on the back of your neck standing to attention. Your skin will be covered in goose bumps. Your heart will be thumping. Before you go out, he'll stand at the dressing room door. No player leaves without him being there pre-match and at half-time. You walk past him and he shakes the hand of every player and every member of staff. He doesn't have to say anything. He's the boss, probably the greatest manager ever in this country. What more motivation do you need?'

Although there is a lot to be gained from becoming aware of the general way in which you talk to yourself, it is easier said than done. But let me give you some ideas about what to look out for and how to keep your self-talk as helpful as possible, because using it effectively is a critical factor in both building and maintaining your confidence to cope with change. There are two steps to doing this.

First, don't try to deny or ignore that there is some degree of concern or negativity in your mind. Former England rugby player Jonny Wilkinson often welcomed the feelings of nerves and worry before a game because it indicated that he was getting himself ready to play rugby. Denying that you have these worries only stops you from taking positive action to control your internal voice. Recognise that a degree of doubt is necessary in order to get you to provide some clear ideas about how you are going to handle things through your own strengths. Once you have recognised what your negative voice sounds like, practise coming up with an alternative that gets you focused on taking action rather than dwelling on negative possibilities. To begin with, you should collect a typical set of negative statements that you regularly use. Once you have identified them, you can practise using a chart like the one below to replace them.

Try this. What is a more effective way of saying each of the following comments?

Negative comment	Positive comment
EXAMPLE: *Don't worry about it. Don't get nervous. Don't panic.*	*Stay calm. Take deep breaths and think clearly.*
Don't think about the audience.	
Don't make any mistakes. Don't cock it up. Don't lose the plot.	
Don't be disappointed. Don't get frustrated.	
Don't say anything controversial.	
Don't feel angry about it. Don't be so upset.	
Don't do anything undisciplined.	
Don't get complacent. Don't get lazy. Don't relax.	
Don't be overconfident. Don't be too cocky.	
Don't let me down.	
Don't read too much into what they say.	
Don't argue with me.	
Don't be afraid to speak up.	

Secondly, you also have to recognise the times when you are saying the wrong things to yourself. Sir Steve Redgrave described how these moments tended to happen to him just before a race. When he started to recognise this, he would give himself a 'mental slap' or what psychologists call *thought stopping*, which is a great technique to consider.

Thought stopping is a mental cue that is used to block out negative thoughts. An image or a word is used to block negative thoughts coming through. The choice of this image or word is completely up to you. Olympic champion Linford Christie used the image of the 'B' of the bang of the starting gun to do it but some athletes use images of a red traffic light, a large STOP road sign, a road block or an emergency stop button. Others prefer to just say 'Stop', either out loud or in their head, to halt the flow of negativity. One athlete I know used the image of the *A-Team*'s Mr T yelling at him! Whatever word or image you use, it can also be effectively paired up with a physical cue at the same time. So, as well as blocking the thought in the head, a clenched fist or clapping your hands together can help shift your focus back on to positive thoughts.

Ferguson looked on with fierce pride when Arsenal captain Patrick Vieira attempted to intimidate his United team in 2005. Vieira had threatened Gary Neville, an act which prompted Roy Keane, the man Ferguson referred to as 'The closest embodiment to myself', to confront his opposing captain in the tunnel. 'Pick on me. Pick on someone your own size,' the Irishman, who stands at five foot ten inches, snarled at the towering Vieira, who is six inches taller. After his team had won, Ferguson seized upon the powerful image and coined a phrase he would employ as his – and the team's – own mental cue. He said: 'There are no wimps in my team.'

Once this thought-stopping technique has worked, following it up quickly with the alternative positive statement from the table above will help get you focused on the positive action to follow. This is very important. Not bringing in the positive thought leaves a vacuum and allows the negativity to come right back again.

Don't use don't

There's an old joke that the comedian Henny Youngman told about staying in a posh hotel where he noticed a sign in the bathroom instructing, 'Do not steal our towels. We will charge you £5 per towel'. He held up one of the towels to inspect it. It was about five feet long and luxuriously thick. He calculated that such a towel would cost him at least £25 at a shop, so he promptly took five of them. 'What a hotel!' he would proclaim. 'The towels were so big and fluffy, I could hardly close my suitcase.'

If you say to yourself (or someone says to you), 'Don't make any mistakes,' then your brain receives a message of what *not* to do, rather than a clear and positive instruction of what action is needed. For example, imagine that you are about to deliver an important presentation under the pressure of a glaring audience. If we have images of making mistakes and stumbling over our words, an unhelpful picture appears which can make it difficult to deliver the presentation flawlessly. We are now worried about failing, as opposed to focusing on succeeding. Consider how the decision-making process is different when the instruction to ourselves is to 'go out there and deliver a calm, assured and polished presentation'. The absence of the 'don't', or more importantly, the presence of the positive instruction, speeds up the thinking process and allows you to focus on delivering a better result. You are clear what is expected and are not caught in two minds or second-guessing yourself.

Sir Alex Ferguson outlined this philosophy in his own unique way. When asked about Manchester United's success, he claimed that it was based on the belief that 'Manchester United never get beaten. We may occasionally run out of time but we never believe we can be beaten.' This mantra was reinforced through the content of the daily training sessions. United's players were also made to practise how they should play if a goal was required with ten, five, or three minutes remaining. 'We practise for when the going gets tough, so we don't panic but instead, know what it takes to be successful in those situations,' said assistant coach Rene Meulensteen.

Affirmations

Psychologists have shown that there are two things which determine how we tend to remember an experience, whether it is dealing with change, going on a holiday or a day at work. These factors are:

a. how the experience felt when it was at its peak (the best or the worst moments)
b. how it felt when it ended

Research has proved that we use these two factors most when we remember an event. It doesn't actually matter what the majority of the experience was like, these factors have the biggest influence over whether we decide to go back and repeat it. The lesson of these intriguing findings is that no matter how stressful or trying the changing circumstances can seem, you should always try to finish on a high note. Great sports coaches understand this and always end a training session in a positive way. Muhammad Ali did it at the end of his most gruelling training sessions by raising his arms in celebration and repeatedly intoning his mantra, 'I am the greatest.' This kept his spirits high and ensured that he continued to train hard. He was using an affirmation, which is a positive statement about your own skills and abilities. Using affirmations during change can keep your confidence levels high. These statements plant positive thoughts in the fertile ground of your mind and make sure that your self-belief in your ability and skills are constantly influenced by a positive perspective.

I once met the former heavyweight boxing champion Mike Tyson, who had a large entourage surrounding him. Tyson admitted that their continual encouragement helped to remind him of his own strengths and abilities. The benefits to his confidence were enormous as they offered a non-stop chorus of how good he was. Can you imagine how it would feel to have a crowd constantly reminding you of your abilities? We would soon end up with a positive view of ourselves, wouldn't we? Having your own affirmations is simply the (cheaper) equivalent of having your own permanent rent-a-crowd.

These reminders are not simply being positive for the sake of it – we have to know that they are truthful and meaningful if they are to have any impact. The comedienne Victoria Wood once returned from a diet class and looked at herself in the mirror. 'All I could see was wrinkles. I looked at my flabby arms. I studied my big hips and my thick thighs. I could only see cellulite everywhere. I turned to my husband and said, "Please say something positive to give me hope." He looked at me for a long time, obviously deep in thought. "At least there's nothing wrong with your eyesight," he said.'

You may think that this is too obvious to be effective. If you're not convinced, try this Jack Dee-inspired exercise for the next few days. The sour-faced comedian jokes that when he wakes up, 'The first thing I do is look in the bathroom mirror, crack a quick smile and get it out of the way for the day.' When you get out of bed in the morning, tell yourself that you feel terrible, that you can't be bothered, and then see how you cope. We have already seen that, given the choice, when left to our own devices, we tend to revert to negative thinking and focus on doubts. We need to ensure that if we are to deal effectively with change, we are making deliberate attempts to counter this.

Make a list of between four and eight statements that relate to positive things about you – for example: *I am calm and confident in the face of change.* You can, of course, update these as often as necessary to ensure that past and present positives are used to underpin confidence. Once these reminders have been identified, write them on a card and read them daily. Eventually the statements will seem easier to repeat with conviction and you will become more comfortable with the whole process of staying positively confident.

Body language

Although I would always suggest that self-talk and thought control exercises are the most effective ways to stay confident during change, there is another way to take control and really stack the confidence odds in your favour. It involves using your body, your body language and your physiology.

Ferguson claims that the best piece of advice he ever received about the media came from Granada TV's one-time head of sport, Paul Doherty, who told him, 'You give the game away at your press conferences. You're showing your worries.' Doherty suggested that Ferguson 'Look in the mirror and put the Alex Ferguson face on when you face the press.' It was advice he took to heart and from then on, he would prepare himself mentally. 'Appearing beleaguered and showing your torments is no way to help the team or improve your chances of winning,' he reasoned.

Former US President Richard Nixon would have understood. Nixon had inadvertently offered some great examples of the importance of body language. In 1960, he took part in the first ever televised presidential debate, where television viewers believed that his opponent, John F. Kennedy, had the better of him. Radio listeners, however, thought that Nixon had won. Why? Before he went on television, Nixon had refused to use make-up and so his face appeared sweaty and anxious throughout the debate. Television viewers had focused on what they saw rather than on what they heard, and so drew an opposite conclusion to radio listeners.

Nixon didn't learn the lessons well, because in 1974, when he gave his resignation speech to the nation after the Watergate scandal, he appeared calm and collected. However, researchers analysing his facial expressions noticed a 'furious rate' of eye blinking (above fifty blinks per minute), suggesting extremely high levels of anxiety. Subsequent analyses of blink rates during eight televised presidential debates have shown that the candidate who blinks the most is more likely to lose the forthcoming election.

If our thoughts are positive but everything about our body is acting negatively (head dropped, shoulders slouched, moving lethargically) then, not surprisingly, it is going to be difficult for our thoughts to have any impact. Therefore, we have to practise changing our body language to help kick-start our confidence. It is useful to be aware of the kind of body language that enables you to do this.

A useful idea when deciding how to adopt positive body language is to identify a role model who displays excellent body language. Choose someone you really admire and then study their body language. During change, when you come to critical moments, take on their body language and benefit from the confidence they have already developed.

Ferguson adopted this approach for himself. In the final training session before every European game, he would wear an old 1960s United jersey, the same kind worn by his hero, Denis Law. 'Law epitomised everything a Scotsman is about. He was daring and courageous, he had that bravado about him and he had style. He was truly fantastic,' Ferguson rhapsodised.

He encouraged the same idea in his players – using outward appearance to bolster an inner sense of capability and pride – by creating an official club dress code. Gary Neville says: 'As captain, I would sometimes ask him before the longer flights whether we could travel in tracksuits. He would say, "You'll wear your club blazer, son. You're walking through an airport, representing Manchester United, so you'll walk tall and proud. Once you're on the plane, you can put your tracksuit on. But at the other end you put your blazer back on."' Wayne Rooney acknowledges the effect of this practice. He says: 'I take great pride in travelling away in a blazer with the badge on your chest. You get off the coach suited and booted and it made me feel bulletproof. We look like we mean business.'

Ferguson also used it as diversionary tactic to avert a crisis of confidence. In April 1996, United were headed towards defeat at Southampton at a particularly crucial point in the title race. At half-time, he decided to make his players change from their grey kit into a more traditional blue and white away strip.

Following the potentially destabilising 3–1 defeat at The Dell, Ferguson told incredulous journalists after the match: 'The players couldn't pick each other out. They said it was difficult to see their team-mates at distance when they lifted their heads. It was nothing to do with superstition.' However, the grey shirts were never to be worn again and United went on to win their next three games to claim their third title in three years.

Write down the names of people whose body language you admire and note what behaviours you could adopt to help you.

In short, success breeds confidence but we also know that confidence breeds success. Take personal responsibility for your levels of confidence and you will be surprised at the results.

Whistle a Happy Tune

Whenever I feel afraid
I hold my head erect
And whistle a happy tune,
So no one will suspect
I'm afraid

While shivering in my shoes
I strike a careless pose
And whistle a happy tune,
And no one ever knows

I'm afraid
The result of this deception
Is very strange to tell,
For when I fool the people I fear
I fool myself as well!

I whistle a happy tune,
And every single time
The happiness in the tune
Convinces me that I'm
Not afraid

Make believe you're brave
And the trick will take you far;
You may be as brave
As you make believe you are.
You may be as brave
As you make believe you are.

Rodgers and Hammerstein, *The King and I*

Control the Winds
of Change

Grant me the serenity to accept the things I cannot change, the courage to change the things I can, and the wisdom to know the difference.

Ralph Waldo Emerson

At the start of March 1996, Newcastle were twelve points clear of United and on course to win their first League title since 1927. However, Kevin Keegan's team were starting to buckle under the weight of expectation and Ferguson began to sense it. Six weeks after United had rattled Newcastle by beating them at their St James's Park home, United were in ruthless and clinical form. They won seven of their matches 1–0 and Eric Cantona scored the winner in five of them. United were catching Newcastle and Ferguson was doing all he could to crank up the pressure.

After United had beaten Leeds at Old Trafford, Ferguson chose to spend his press conference musing on the commitment Leeds had demonstrated. He suggested that if Leeds had replicated that kind of passion throughout the season, they would not be in the poor League position in which they currently found themselves. Towards the end, Ferguson casually lobbed a hand grenade, saying: 'I hope Leeds will show the same kind of determination when they play Newcastle at Elland Road in twelve days' time.' He stood back and waited for the explosion.

Twelve days later, Newcastle beat Leeds, and after the game Kevin Keegan donned his earphones, stared straight into the Sky cameras and delivered the quivering diatribe of a doomed man that will forever be the epitaph of Newcastle's 1995–96 season.

'I think you have to send a tape of the game to Alex Ferguson,' Keegan said, his voice breaking with emotion. 'Isn't that Leeds performance what he wants? You just don't say that about Leeds. I would love it if we could beat them [United]. He's gone down a lot in my estimation. Football in this country is honest. You sometimes wonder about abroad but not in this country. I would love it if we beat them. Love it.'

Ferguson was publicly unrepentant. 'I was stopped dead in my tracks by Kevin's outburst,' he said. 'God, I felt for him. Looking at replays later, I was better able to digest what he said and at first it made me feel a bit guilty. Then I thought to myself that I had done nothing wrong. I had said something about the honesty of the game, which I had a right to do.'

Nevertheless, what Ferguson had accomplished, intentionally or not, was the public psychological dismemberment of his greatest rival that season. He ruthlessly exposed how vulnerable and emotionally fragile Keegan was. At that point everyone – including the Newcastle players – knew United had the title in the bag. And Ferguson's ability to manipulate his rivals came to be regarded as being as significant as anything that happened on the pitch. The press had a new concept to play with. It was from that point on that managerial mind games became part of the football lexicon.

You must be choking!

Accusing someone of 'choking' or 'bottling it' are two of the biggest insults in the sports world, which is why they are banned in many sporting dressing rooms, where the ability to cope with pressure is seen as essential. It is what sets the professionals apart from those of us who left our composure behind on school sports day. However, there is also research to suggest that banning this kind of talk is important.

Harvard University conducted a simple experiment. Two groups were asked to complete a basketball shooting challenge. Before they began, they were separately given their instructions, which were identical except for one thing. The second group were told, just as they were about to go out and perform, about 'choking' and told that performance levels suffered a catastrophic drop when choking occurred. They were told not to choke when they began their exercise.

The results?

Well, if you read the advice in the previous chapter about not using the term 'Don't', it will be no surprise that the second group, which had been given information about choking, delivered a significantly inferior performance to that of the other group. The mere thought of choking had been enough to make a difference.

So what exactly is choking?

It is best explained by understanding its effects, which may be likened to the way a boa constrictor kills. The snake winds its body around its prey and each time the victim breathes out, the boa constrictor tightens its hold slightly. The prey can't inhale as deeply on the next breath. Every time it breathes out it can't breathe in as much. Soon it can't breathe in at all and suffocation follows shortly afterwards.

Choking is like this. It is a normal human reaction, especially when we are facing the pressures of change, because it is our natural response to a perceived threat. To demonstrate what choking is (don't worry; not literally), try 'The breathless test'.

Get someone you know to stand up, then explain that you are going to test their reaction time. Explain how you will watch them carefully and assess how quickly they respond to your commands. Then begin barking verbal commands. 'Look left … look right … look left … look up … look left … look left … look right …' As you continue the task and get increasingly quicker, the participant's anxiety levels will start to increase. Watch how their breathing patterns now begin to change. Without realising it, many people in this situation will start to hold their breath.

This is a mistake. Oxygen is energy. It helps your muscles relax and clears your mind. When you hold your breath, you create pressure and the feeling of nerves. The great 400-metre runner Michael Johnson describes anxiety as 'Excitement without the breath'. The pattern of your breathing affects how you perform. When you are under stress, deep breathing helps bring your mind and body back to the present.

Have you ever stepped into a cold shower or icy lake? The cold takes your breath away and your first impulse is to get out. But if you breathe and stay focused, you gradually become accustomed to the water temperature. The experience is akin to performing under pressure. By breathing and focusing you can systematically desensitise yourself.

Try this simple three-step breathing technique:

1. Remain still and focus on calming your body and mind. It helps to try and relax your fingertips and your toes.
2. Breathe deeply through the nose and out through the mouth according to the following routine.
3. Inhale through the nose: count to four.
4. Exhale through the mouth: count to four.
5. (Repeat as often as necessary.)
6. Before refocusing on the outside world, repeat silently one of your affirmations, such as 'I feel calm' or 'I know I can cope'.

Control the controllables

In addition to changing our breathing patterns, when we are under stress our focus turns inwards. In the chapter on confidence, we looked at how we begin to think about the things that won't help us and how this can impair our limited focus. For example, golfers who focus on not landing in the bunker and presenters worrying about fluffing their lines often end up doing those very things.

The old adage about 'controlling the controllables' is unquestionably the most commonly used phrase in the world of sports psychology, but that does not mean it isn't true. Research suggests that you will remember about 5 per cent of the content of this book in a month's time, so I will give you the same advice I often share with others facing change. If you only remember one thing in this book, be sure to remember this one phrase: control the controllables. It is invaluable.

Why waste your energy, effort and resources in worrying or getting angry about uncontrollable factors such as technology, inferior equipment or the experience of others? Instead focus on the things that you can do something about. When you're getting ready to face change, you must identify what the controllable factors actually are. The legendary swimming coach Bob Bowman would deliberately arrange practices that made his protégé, Michael Phelps, uncomfortable, including altering practice times at late notice, cancelling taxis to take him home and banning him from drinking water in his breaks. He once purposely stepped on Phelps's swimming goggles just moments before a race, forcing him to make do without them.

Bowman defined an Olympic champion as someone who can deal with any event that comes their way, and he said, 'You have to behave like an Olympic champion long before there's a gold medal around your neck.'

At the 2008 Olympic Games in Beijing, Phelps was racing in the final of the 200 metres butterfly, which would bring him the fourth of his eight gold medals. Moments after he dived into the pool, Phelps's goggles began to leak, effectively rendering him blind. At this moment, the years of Bob Bowman's 'control the controllables' training kicked in. He accepted that he could only control his reaction and adapted his stroke pattern to win the race in a world record time.

Sir Alf Ramsey, England's World Cup-winning manager, was once asked about how he was able to get his players to fully understand his vision of how he wanted the game to be played. His reply:

> Constant repetition gets the message home.
> Constant repetition gets the message home.
> Constant repetition gets the message home.
> Constant repetition gets the message home.
> Constant repetition gets the message home.
> Constant repetition gets the message home.

Sir Alex Ferguson incorporated this same principle into his own training methods. Throughout the year, training sessions were focused on repetition of skills and tactics. 'Some managers are "pleasing managers". They let the players play eight-a-sides or ten-a-sides — games they enjoy. But here, we look at the training sessions as opportunities to learn and improve. Sometimes the players may think "Here we go again," but it helps to win when we are under pressure. The message is simple: we cannot sit still at this club.'

This theme was also central to Ferguson's half-time talks to the players. 'You have maybe eight minutes to deliver your message, so it is vital to use the time well,' he says. 'You can talk about concentrating and the small things you can address. But when you are losing, you have to make an impact. I liked to focus on our own team and our own strengths in order to correct why you are losing.'

It's like going for your driving test. Many drivers get nervous about the experience and worry about which manoeuvres they will be asked to perform, whether the car will feel familiar and how nice the examiner will be. When you begin to outline these concerns, it becomes clear that you cannot control what the examiner will be like or what you'll be asked to do. There are, however, quite a few things which you can control. Decide on just three. For example:

1. Take a few deep breaths before sitting in the car to calm down.
2. Slow down and drive at a steady pace.
3. Make an effort to enjoy the whole experience.

As Michael Phelps's example illustrated, this is exactly what great athletes do under pressure. They identify a few key controllables and then focus entirely on them. Whilst interviewing rowers at the 1996 Olympics, US sports commentator Charlie Jones spoke to a number of the competing athletes. Any time he asked them a question about something which was outside their control (like the weather, the strengths and weaknesses of their opponents or what might go wrong during a race), the Olympians would respond with the phrase, 'That's outside my boat.' Gary Neville echoes this message. 'I never heard the word "unlucky" mentioned in twenty years in our dressing room. We had a saying that "We make our own luck".'

This was something Ferguson was reminded of when he sat watching John Terry start his run-up to take the penalty that could have won the Champions League for Chelsea in 2008. 'I thought we were done,' Ferguson says. 'I thought we were done, and I was determined to retain my dignity in defeat.

'When Ashley Cole took their second-last penalty, I clasped my hands, and I prayed. Van der Sar' – United's goalkeeper – 'nearly saved it but once the ball went in, I said to myself, "Don't ever pray again." Because when I was in my first cup final as manager of Aberdeen we were 1–0 up, and Rangers scored two goals in the last two minutes of injury time … I had prayed as well, that day, and I thought I would never do it again. They beat us 2–1, even though I had prayed to God.' When Terry was lining up his kick, Ferguson recalls, 'I watched him walk up and I said, "He'll blast it. I'm sure he'll blast it." Then he goes to side-foot it, and he slips.' By refusing to focus on anything beyond their control, these champions were able to bring all their energy to bear on what was within their control. In your own life, focusing exclusively on what's 'in your boat' not only increases your effectiveness, but dramatically reduces your levels of stress.

As the baseball legend Babe Ruth once said: 'I'm not going to worry about the things I can't control, because if I can't control them there's no point in worrying about them; and I'm not going to worry about the things I can control, because if I can control them there's no point in worrying about them.'

Take a really close look at the change situation you are facing and figure out exactly what you can and cannot control. It's worth writing these things down. Make a list like the one below:

SITUATION	CONTROLLABLES	NON-CONTROLLABLES

Changing the Goalposts

Obstacles are those frightful things you see when you take your eyes off your goal.

Henry Ford

'Winning championships is Manchester United's trade. Sir Alex Ferguson understands the business of winning them in every possible detail,' said Steve Bruce, the former United captain. This was especially true on a sodden May afternoon in Wigan, when Manchester United came seeking a victory that would secure the 2008 Premier League title. 'It was a difficult game,' the United manager says. 'It was an away game and the conditions also made it tough.' United had to win because anything less might have afforded closest rivals Chelsea victory in the title race instead.

Cristiano Ronaldo's opening goal from the penalty spot was not sufficient to induce a mood of technical-area serenity. 'When it remained at 1–0, we had some nervous moments and when the rain came, anything could have happened then,' Ferguson admits. 'I was thinking, "Please give me a second goal."' Instead, it was Wigan's powerful forward, Emile Heskey, who came closest to scoring. He put a header just wide of the goal. As he watched the opportunity go begging, he punched the turf in frustration. 'I knew it was a good chance,' the player later admitted.

It was a small, seemingly insignificant moment to the twenty-five thousand or so spectators, and to the millions of television viewers watching on. To Ferguson, it was an important detail. He noted that the grass came loose beneath Heskey's fist and immediately instructed substitute Ryan Giggs to get ready to go on. 'Heskey's punch showed me that the ground was soft and so Ryan's pace would be crucial,' Ferguson explains. Ten minutes later, Wayne Rooney looked up, measured the space and slid the ball through a gaping central defensive hole into which Giggs cantered. The 34-year-old steadied himself before slipping a finish beyond the goalkeeper to record their second goal. Manchester United would be crowned Premier League champions for the tenth time.

'Would you tell me, please, which way I ought to go from here?' said Alice.

'That depends a good deal on where you want to get to,'
said the Cat.
'I don't care much where,' said Alice.
'Then it doesn't matter which way you go,' said the Cat.

Lewis Carroll, *Alice in Wonderland*

This quote is a great example of how many of us set goals. Following the *Alice in Wonderland* method can have an adverse impact on how you cope during change. It means that when you come under pressure, you lose focus or become derailed. Setting goals will help you make sense of what you are trying to achieve and allows you to stay in control even in the most trying of circumstances.

Edwin Locke and Gary Latham are two professors who have spent years studying thousands of top performers and they have discovered that all these people set themselves goals. In fact, they estimate that an effective goal can improve performance by up to 16 per cent (the equivalent of saving yourself an hour in an average eight-hour day). Sir Alex Ferguson's approach to goal setting, as detailed in that victory at Wigan, where he maintained his focus on the process of winning and allowed the score – and title – to take care of itself, is a great introduction to a simple framework useful when facing change. It is a goal-setting framework which distinguishes between outcome, performance and process goals.

Another legendary coach, LA Lakers' Phil Jackson, provides an excellent example of how these three types of goals work: 'For the first thirty-six minutes of every forty-minute basketball game, I avoid checking the scoreboard (performance goal), and instead maintain my complete focus on helping the players to perform well (process goal). Only in the last four minutes of the game do I become concerned with the outcome because I know that by then, my team will have won the game with a superior performance.'

Outcome goals relate to the final result – the bigger picture. 'A few months after I first arrived at Manchester United in November 1986,' Ferguson recalls, 'Bobby Charlton and I travelled to Barcelona to try to get Mark Hughes back. We walked around the stadium in the morning. We visited their amazing training facilities. If there was an injury, there were invariably five or six people – doctors, physios, witch doctors, everything – available.' In contrast, Ferguson adds, 'We had a man with a sponge. Charlton turned to me and said: "You know – this is where we should be. We should be at this level, but we aren't – and it's crazy. When you look through the past forty years of our history, back to the Busby Babes and all of those great teams, it should be the case." Then he said: "Let's think about achieving that. Let's think about being better than the European elite, like Barcelona."'

Creating this outcome goal set a positive theme for the future and offered a clear direction and destination which everyone could move towards. It was Ferguson's equivalent of the North Star, which the captain of a ship uses to set his vessel's course.

When he retired in 2013, Ferguson was asked to name his greatest signing. He recounted his conversation in Barcelona with Sir Bobby Charlton and proudly singled out not a player, but the club's Carrington training facility, to which they had moved in 2000. He cited the reaction of those who saw it. 'All players arrive here and say, "Wow, this is some training ground." It's one of the best in the world, and I think if any player were to come here with any doubts about where they should be, they'll soon find out that this is a fantastic set-up.'

Performance goals refer to the numbers (in sport that is points, times or distances; in business it could be targets for sales, turnover, retention rates, etc.) required to achieve the outcome. One of Ferguson's most famous lines is his 2002 assertion during an interview that 'My greatest challenge was knocking Liverpool off their fucking perch. And you can print that.' Despite the emotional language, it is a great illustration of Ferguson's ability to set clear performance goals for his team.

Before Ferguson won his first League title in 1993, United had been crowned as the best team in the land on seven occasions to Liverpool's eighteen. Setting his outcome goal as making United the world's best club, Ferguson used Liverpool's achievement as his performance goal. He communicated this to all who played for him. Gary Neville sums up his reaction to this ambitious aim: 'I loathed Liverpool and I loathed their success. I wanted to beat that target.' Ferguson enjoyed the moment when he passed the figure and eventually took United's grand total to twenty titles. He then encouraged the club to recalibrate its European title targets. 'We should have won more than three European Cups,' he announced. 'We need to be closer to five or six.'

Process goals are the controllable behaviours you need to engage in to deliver the performance goals. These can include tactics and strategy as well as your attitude. It was Ferguson's ruthless focus on achieving his process goals whilst moving in the right direction that saved his job early in his tenure at United and underpinned the eventual success he would bring to the club. By the end of the 1988–89 season, all he had to show for two years of toil and frustration was a runners-up slot to Liverpool. 'His team seemed to have no shape, no purpose, no direction and he had no apparent idea what to do about it. Nothing made sense,' writes former winger Willie Morgan.

Sports writer and Manchester United fan Jim White recalls: 'By the autumn of that year, the lads on the terraces had turned on him. He claimed to have a master plan, but all they could see was a Scottish whinger with an inflated reputation for doing things in the small world north of the border.' Old Trafford icon George Best declared that he wouldn't 'walk around the corner to see [United] play'.

By January 1990, after a run of eight games without a victory, United were fifth from bottom in the League and Ferguson was, it appeared from the outside, about to be seeking new employment. *Manchester Evening News* journalist David Meek compared him to a prisoner on death row in America: 'The man has been condemned in so many quarters, and is being kept alive by a succession of appeals.' According to Bobby Charlton, however, the board was not to be persuaded by press campaigns or fan pressure. 'During that time we never, ever, discussed Alex Ferguson's position,' Sir Bobby maintains. 'Because we knew what he was doing was right.' It was the small series of process goals that he was achieving that reassured his employers and retained their faith. He was in his office by 7.30 a.m. every day, restructuring the youth system, working on the reserves, training with the first team, negotiating with other managers, constantly looking for hints of transfer-list action, scouting school games in the afternoons, watching other teams in the evenings, back home at midnight and poring over videos until two or three in the morning.

One wonderful example had come in November 1987. On his fourteenth birthday, the doorbell rang at Ryan Giggs's home in Swinton. It was Alex Ferguson himself, there to ask Lynne Giggs whether her eldest son would sign schoolboy forms for United. 'If the manager of Manchester United comes round to your house,' Giggs later said, 'you tend to be a bit flattered. It's a rather nice feeling and not the kind of offer you turn down.' Twenty-one years after his manager's visit, Giggs's goal against Wigan moved Ferguson closer to his performance and outcome goals by drawing United level with Liverpool's title haul of eighteen and cementing the club among Europe's elite.

GOAL TYPES

We can summarise this goal-setting framework as follows:

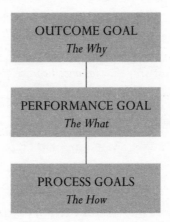

This simple framework can be used in the commercial world when putting together annual business plans and the principles can easily be applied to setting goals for a team. However, for the purposes of this book let's look at how to use it to deal with the pressures of change.

Dame Kelly Holmes won her first Olympic gold medal by using this approach. First she identified the *outcome goal*, which was to win the Olympic 800 metres final in Athens. This extract from her training diary captures what it meant to her:

1 January 2004

I have dreamed forever to be the best at what I do. Some dreams come true, but my biggest ones are still out there and I really want them to become reality. I have really gone through a lot to realise my dreams. I have the passion, dedication, willpower and heart to achieve my ultimate goals. I have put my life and soul into this, given up my life to pursue what I know is my destiny. I just pray that for once I can be given the lift to get through this year with no struggles, no injuries and a lighted spirit of guidance. I hope 2004 can bring me more happiness, success and purpose than ever before.

Obviously, this incredibly challenging goal was realistic for her, but it didn't tell her what she needed to do to actually achieve it. So, with her coach, she analysed and studied previous results, the current form of her opposition and her own capabilities to figure out that running the distance in one minute and fifty-eight seconds should be enough to win the gold medal. She now had her *performance goal*, a more specific target.

Nevertheless, Holmes went one stage further and assessed how she was going to run the final in this time. She eventually focused on just three *process goals*, including remaining calm, ensuring that she stayed out of the pack, and practising her final 'kick' in the home straight. These goals were all completely within her control.

When she was finally ready to perform under the eyes of the world, where do you think her focus was? It wasn't on winning the gold medal (despite this being the reason she was there). Nor was it on running the race in one minute and fifty-eight seconds. She focused on her process goals, the three controllable things that she knew would impact upon her performance. These process goals gave her the confidence she needed and helped her avoid getting carried away with the pressure and intensity of the event. She described this approach as 'Going back to basics'. It means getting the basic performance right and letting the outcome take care of itself.

One teacher I know used a simple exercise to emphasise the same point to an unruly class of children. Standing by the door and looking nine metres across the room to the window, she asked them: 'Who believes that I can jump from one side of the room to the other?' There was stunned silence and looks of disbelief, followed by an uncertain chorus of 'No.'

Eventually, one child said, 'Of course you can't, unless you are the world long jump champion.'

'I can,' she said, 'and what's more, I believe that you can too.' Again, there were looks of utter disbelief, but now she had their complete attention. She then began to jump, half a metre, followed by another half metre, and another, and another, and so on until she reached the window. She turned to the class and said, 'See – any of you could jump across this room. Goal setting is like that too. We will take it one step at a time until we have made it all the way to our final outcome. Are you with me?' There was a chorus of 'Yes,' and a roomful of smiles.

So how can you break down your goals for surviving change into similar smaller steps?

The Shakespeare Principle

Before we begin to set our goals, we should first take a lesson from diamond experts. Do you know how these experts are able to spot a fake diamond? It is easy. The fakes are perfect whereas all real diamonds have flaws. Perfectionist thinking, when combined with goal setting, tends to make it easy to define your results as a failure unless you get it exactly right. Not only does this stop you from analysing what you have learned ('what's the point?'), it also de-motivates you from trying again.

To avoid falling into this trap, try thinking about employing the Shakespeare Principle when setting goals.

Let me ask you a simple question: How many of Shakespeare's plays can you name? Have a go and write down as many as you can think of.

How did you do? Did you get close to naming all major works which the bard produced? Most people struggle to name even a quarter of them. Shakespeare wrote a number of plays which had varying levels of commercial success when they were first produced. The Shakespeare Principle, therefore, suggests that when setting your goals, you should try to use a range of criteria to define your own success. These are:

a. Dream result
b. Realistic result
c. Minimum acceptable result

For example, Shakespeare wrote the celebrated *Hamlet* one year and then produced the not nearly so successful *Troilus and Cressida* the next. Despite the fact that not every one of his plays was a commercial hit, it didn't stop him continuing to write. The dream result refers to everything going as well as possible, like having a perfect day with everything falling into place. The realistic result refers to a level of performance that you know will be very satisfactory, if all goes well.

The minimum acceptable result refers to the level of performance that you are unwilling to drop below. Anything lower than this and you will feel that you have not done yourself justice.

Tips on setting your goals

There are some other important tips to note about goal setting, especially when writing down your top-level outcome goals.

1 First person

Psychologists estimate that we spend as much as 90 per cent of our time modifying our behaviour to fit in to certain situations. For example, a recent survey asked businessmen which facilities were most influential in their choice of one hotel over another. At the top of the list came the presence of a hotel gym, with 70 per cent of respondents indicating that it was a very important factor in their thinking. On the basis of such a finding, many hotels began expanding their gym facilities. The reality, though, is that just 17 per cent of hotel residents actually ever use the gym.

When setting your own goals, make sure they genuinely appeal to you and aren't just what you think sounds great to others. Additionally, when writing down your goals, it is important to pay attention to your choice of words as they contain clues about your true intentions and desires. You must own your goals and be able to clearly associate yourself with them.

Paul Britton, the criminal psychologist, believes that our language contains lots of unconscious clues. In tests to establish whether an individual is lying, one common giveaway is a reluctance to refer to themselves, whereas in normal conversation we do tend to refer to ourselves a lot. Liars try to avoid including lots of first person references, such as 'I', 'me', 'my', and instead use terms such as 'everyone' and 'no one'. They are placing a distance between themselves and the lie.

Write your goals for you and you alone.

2 Present tense

'This time next year, we'll be millionaires!'

This one phrase, frequently uttered by the hapless wheeler-dealer Del Boy Trotter to his brother Rodney in the television series, *Only Fools and Horses*, is the reason why it took them so long to realise their own dreams of riches. He would have been far better talking about it as if it had already happened. In other words, had the television character of Del been real, he should have acted 'as if' he already was a multi-millionaire. The actor Cary Grant, whose real name was Archie Leach, understood this. He said, 'I pretended to be somebody I wanted to be, until I finally became that person. Or he became me.'

Tests have shown that getting children to work in the first person and in the present tense is a highly effective method of learning. For example, asking students to imagine what it must have been like to be Winston Churchill during the Second World War, or Queen Elizabeth I resisting the Spanish invasion, and how they might have thought through the options open to them, is a very effective approach to engagement. This is because our subconscious mind, the storage part of our brain, thinks only in the present tense.

The composer Benjamin Zander uses the same approach in teaching musical performance. He was frustrated by how his students felt anxiety about gaining high marks rather than focusing on enjoying the beauty of the music. He decided, therefore, that he would award every student an A grade for the course before it had even started. The one criterion for achieving this was that every student had to write a letter – dated for the end of the year ahead – which began 'Dear Mr Zander, I got an A because ...' In this letter, they had to tell, in as much detail as possible, the story of what had happened to them during the year to enable them to achieve this grade. Give yourself an A and imagine that you have already achieved your goal before you even start.

3 Specific

You must be very specific about what you want to achieve. At the very first Olympic triathlon competition in the Sydney 2000 Games, Canadian athlete Simon Whitfield achieved a remarkable victory by applying this approach. He was in second place in the run (the final event after the swim and cycle stages) by a seemingly insurmountable distance. With such a substantial lead nearing the finish, German athlete Stefan Vuckovic started to look back several times, to ensure that the pack was not converging to knock him out of a medal position. However, Whitfield seemed to explode over the final 400 metres to somehow catch the front-running German just metres before the finish line. As Whitfield flew past him, Vuckovic maintained his pace and celebrated on a par with Whitfield. In the interviews after the race, Vuckovic explained that his vision had been to win a medal – he didn't care what colour. Whitfield, however, said that he had given 100 per cent effort to the very end because he never lost sight of his own vision to have a gold medal hanging around his neck.

4 Emotive

Try this quick exercise.

Think of a dog.

Done it? Now, I suspect it's likely that the dog you thought about has some kind of emotional connection to you. It may have been a cherished family pet, the dog you played with as a kid or a cartoon character you loved watching. Whatever your answer, the reason you did this can be explained by research about how we remember information.

In the 1960s, Dr Albert Mehrabian, a professor at the University College of Los Angeles, gave us the digits 55, 38 and 7. He found that our thoughts could be classified as 55 per cent visual and emotional, 38 per cent vocal (such things as tone of voice and rhythm) and 7 per cent verbal (meaning the actual words used). Therefore, 93 per cent of our memories are non-verbal. So don't spend hours searching for long, clever-sounding words but instead write a goal which speaks to your emotions.

5 No comparisons

Imagine that you have been selected to represent your country in the Olympic Games. You compete, do very well and win a bronze medal. How happy do you think that would make you feel? I bet most of us would be overjoyed and proud of our achievement. Now imagine turning the clock back and competing at the same Olympic Games a second time. This time you do even better and win a silver medal. How happy do you think you would feel this time? Surely we would feel happier after winning the silver medal than the bronze? This is not surprising since the medals are a reflection of our performance and the silver means that you gave a better performance than when winning the bronze. Research, however, tells a different story. Athletes who win bronze medals are happier than those who win silver, and the reason for this has to do with the way in which they think about their performance.

The silver medallists focus on the notion that, if they had performed slightly better, then they would have won a gold medal. In contrast, the bronze medallists focus on the thought that if they had performed slightly worse, then they wouldn't have won anything at all. This tendency to imagine what might have happened, rather than what actually did happen, is known as 'counter-factual thinking'. Let me show you how we are all prey to this kind of thinking.

Imagine that you decide to buy a new calculator. You go to the shop, where the assistant shows you a range of choices. After careful consideration, you choose a model that costs £20. At this point, the assistant looks slightly anxious and explains that the following day the shop is going to have a sale. If you come back then, the calculator will only cost £5. Do you buy a calculator then and there or go back the following day?

Now let's imagine a slightly different scenario. This time you decide to buy a new computer. You go in, and the assistant shows you a range of machines. After much careful consideration, you choose a computer costing £999. Once again, the assistant looks anxious and explains that the following day there will be a sale. If you come back then, the computer will be reduced to £984. Do you buy the computer or return the following day?

Researchers examining the psychology of decision-making have presented these two scenarios to lots of people. In both instances, people have the opportunity to save identical amounts of money and so it would be rational to treat them in exactly the same way. People should either buy the calculator and computer straight away or, if they want to save £15, return the next day. Most people treat the two scenarios very differently. About 70 per cent of people say that they would be put off buying the calculator until the next day but purchase the computer there and then.

Even without a calculator, it is clear that the figures don't add up. Why do so many people act in an irrational way? It seems that we don't view our potential saving in absolute terms but rather as a percentage of the amount of money we are spending. In absolute terms, each time we stand to save £15. This represents 75 per cent of the price of the calculator but just 1.5 per cent of the price of the computer.

Seen in relative terms, the former appears a much better deal and so is well worth waiting for.

When writing your goals to help you successfully come through change, don't just compare yourself to others. Instead, write down what a successful outcome will mean for you.

6 Documented

The Amway Corporation, one of America's most profitable direct-selling companies, encourages its sales force to reach great heights by providing the following advice:

> One final tip before you get started: set a goal and write it down. Whatever the goal, the important thing is that you set it, so you've got something for which to aim – and that you write it down. There is something magical about writing things down. So set a goal and write it down. When you reach that goal, set another and write that down. You'll be off and running.

Why does writing down our goals mean that we will be effective in strengthening our commitment, even when the content of our goals stays private?

Put simply, goals that are written down have more staying power than those that aren't.

How will you document your goal?

Take a piece of paper and write down your goal now.

Review

In the opening chapter, I suggested that you should start to think like Sir Alex Ferguson. It is essential that when you do, you begin to review your own goals regularly. This is the most important part of the whole process of goal setting, because if you don't review your goals, how can you learn what worked and what didn't? A decent rule of thumb is to spend twice as long reviewing your goals as you do setting them. If you are going to get your next goals set at the right level to maximise your motivation, learning and confidence, then you need to give yourself time to assess your efforts.

I know that it is easy to skip this section and start to focus on the next challenge ahead of you, but ask yourself some of the following questions to make sure that you have the right starting point for your next goal.

1. How well did I do what I said I would do? Did I put my goals into action?
2. How successful was I at achieving my goals?
3. What worked well in helping me to achieve my goals?

4.   What did not work so well and detracted from my success?
5.   What main reasons would I give for my success?
6.   What changes would I make to the goals I set based on the result?
7.   How will I make sure I get the same or better level of success with my next goals?

Use goal setting as a skill and see how great you can become at setting, achieving and reviewing your goals. I guarantee that it will help you to start controlling the controllables of change.

One day a human went to heaven in the way that humans often do. On arrival, the human was greeted by a host of angels and given a tour of all of heaven's wonders. Over the course of the tour, the human noticed that there was one room which the angels quickly glided past each time they approached.

'What's in that room?' the human asked.

The angels looked at each other as if they had been dreading the question. Finally, one of them stepped forward and said kindly: 'We're not allowed to keep you out but please believe us – you don't want to go in there.'

The human's mind raced at the thought of what might be contained in that room. What could be so horrible that all the angels of heaven would want to hide it away? The human knew that one should probably take the angels at their word, but found it very hard to resist temptation. 'After all,' the human thought, 'I'm only human.'

Slowly walking towards the room, the human was filled with dread and wonder at what horrors might be about to be revealed. But in fact, the room was filled with the most wonderful things imaginable: a beautiful home; nice things; great wisdom; a happy family; loving friends; and riches beyond measure.

Eyes wide, the human turned back to the angels: 'But why didn't you want me to come in here? This room is filled with the most amazing things I've ever seen.'

The angels looked at each other sadly, then back at the human.

'These are all the things you were meant to have while you were on earth, but you never believed or took steps so you could have them.'

Change Your Mind

There is nothing either good or bad, but thinking makes it so.
William Shakespeare, *Hamlet*

In 1993, after ending United's 26-year wait to win the League title, Alex Ferguson had spent the summer months plotting his strategy to repeat the triumph. If the victorious players were expecting to have an easier ride this time around, they were in for a shock. As the squad began their preparations, Ferguson welcomed them back and began, according to centre half Gary Pallister, by praising them for the way they had conducted themselves under the intense pressure of the season's closing months.

'But having patted us on the back,' Pallister recalls, 'he revealed that he was disturbed by a nagging doubt about the future. He knew he had a great squad with all the quality needed to lift the game's great prizes.

But was it possible, he asked us, that there were some of us who were content to rest on their laurels, who felt that the job had been done now that the title had finally been won? Did everybody in the room have the desire, the raw hunger to go on, to do it again, and again, and again?'

Having posed the question, as United's then captain Bryan Robson recalls, 'He then came up with his masterstroke. He told us: "I've got a sealed envelope in my office drawer. In it is a piece of paper on which I've written down the names of all the players who I think might be satisfied with last year's success, and who might not have what it takes to go on again. It might make interesting reading at the end of the season." With that he took a long, hard look around the dressing room, and he walked out.'

The first reaction of the players, according to Pallister, 'was to have a good laugh about it. But pretty soon somebody said: "Who do you think he's got on that list, then?" Straight away he had got it into our collective psyche that we had a lot of work to do, because nobody wanted to be shown up as a name in his envelope in ten months' time.' Robson testified to the effect of the tactic: 'I don't know if he thought this one up himself, or whether he had learned it from somebody else. What I do know is that it was mightily effective as it helped us win the League and cup double.' Steve Bruce agreed: 'To play for him, you have to have, and be, a certain type of mindset. And if you can't stand up to him then he knows that you're not strong enough to play for Manchester United.'

You have to have a certain type of mindset. Nine words that cut right to the heart of Ferguson's approach.

The way you think about a situation has a huge influence on how much stress you feel. Professor Richard Lazarus, an expert on dealing with stress during change, suggests that we are most vulnerable when we feel that we lack the resources to cope. This may sound obvious but the implication is quite profound. It is not just what is happening around us that can cause us to feel stressed but also the way in which we view it. Therefore, if we can change the way we view a stressful situation, and increase our belief that we can cope, then we will worry less about the impact of change.

So, how do we do it?

We can change our view of a situation in three different ways. To understand this, let's think what it is that we assess when we face potentially stressful changes. Think about deliberating over whether to apply for a new job where you currently work. Although you would really love this new job you're also aware that it is a big step up and you are not sure that your boss will support your application. Are you really good enough to get the job? Whilst the prospect of success is very appealing, what if you don't even make it to the shortlist? Will your confidence be dented? Will your colleagues think you are arrogant for even presuming to apply? What if you do get an interview but freeze when you get in there and ruin any hopes of future appointments? Do you take the risk?

There are lots of questions, but we can simplify what is actually happening in your mind by looking at the three following areas:

1 Demands

'At Manchester United we have to be better than everyone else,' Ferguson once said. 'We set our own standards of behaviour. That is why we work so hard on mindset.'

Ferguson understood the different demands that came from the status of playing for Manchester United. 'There is always somebody wanting a part of your life,' he told author and expert on all things Manchester United Richard Kurt, 'so you have to make sure what you are doing is a priority. And, to me, the priorities are simple. Winning football is all that matters.'

Former youth team player Febian Brandy recalls, 'I was about thirteen when Kieran Richardson [a London-born player who had progressed through the club's ranks] had just made the first team squad. He came into training one day with the car roof down and his music blaring out. He thought he was the man.

Unfortunately for him Fergie was walking into the car park. He pointed at him and said, "Turn your music off and go home. Don't come back here today."' Richardson was sold within two years.

'There is nothing too difficult to understand here, really, as long as you remember what the agenda is,' Ferguson said. 'You only make it difficult for yourself if you go down the wrong road of forgetting how you got here. And part of that is about keeping your feet on the ground. That is part of my job, at least on the football side of things. Sure, you get a few who get carried away elsewhere, but that will never be allowed to interfere with the football side, I can assure you.'

2 Ability

Former United forward Brian McClair once told David Meek of his first meeting with Ferguson in Monaco. McClair was a Celtic player at the time, and was receiving an award as Europe's top goal scorer. He says, '[Ferguson] was there representing Aberdeen, and after the dinner and presentations he asked me what I was going to do. I told him I was going to take the opportunity of being in Monte Carlo by going to the famous casino, to which he said, "Oh no you're not, son, you are going to your bed."

'The funny thing was even though I didn't play for his club and he wasn't my manager, that's exactly what

I did. You accept that what he says is right. Even so, that first experience of meeting him has never left me.' When asked a few years ago to reflect on how Ferguson shaped him, Gary Neville was unequivocal: 'Keep going, hard work, investing in your ability. Sir Alex Ferguson is just relentless.' Neville recalls a dressing-room dressing down after United lost the 1993 Youth Cup final to Leeds. 'He had a little bit of a go at us … a lot of a go. "You've no chance of playing at this club if you're gonna perform like that."' And it is this aspect that enabled Ferguson to demand such high standards of everyone else. 'He taught me the difference between going through the motions or getting everything out of your talent,' says Ole Gunnar Solskjaer.

3 Consequences

'If you lose and Sir Alex believes you gave your best, it's not a problem,' former player Andy Cole once explained. 'But if you lose [in a] limp way … then mind your ears! There are no degrees of anger, no scale: when he loses his temper, he loses his temper.' Cole added: 'He will make it abundantly clear that is not what he expects at United, and then move on.' Ferguson says: 'There is nothing wrong with losing your temper, as long as you do it for the right reasons. My reasons were always about not reaching a certain standard. Then I would let them know.'

In the summer of 1999, United's treble winners went on a pre-season tour to Australia and Hong Kong. Ferguson didn't travel on the first stage of the tour and left assistant Steve McClaren in charge, which meant that some of the squad took advantage. 'We had a few good nights out and broke the curfew that had been put on us,' grins Nicky Butt. 'Once, we stayed out until four in the morning in Sydney. We got away with it but Dwight Yorke got caught coming in at five o'clock.' The following day United had a training session at Sydney's Olympic Stadium. 'We were stretching on the floor, and then I heard someone snoring. It was Yorkey. He'd fallen asleep. Everyone was giggling, but nobody woke him up. He was fast asleep, but he was still sat up. After four or five minutes of stretching, we got up to jog, leaving him asleep in the middle of the field.

'The story got back to the manager,' remembers Butt, 'who came out a few days later. He went nuts.' By the end of that season – only his second at the club – Dwight Yorke admits that Ferguson had told him he was 'failing' and the striker never again hit the heights of 1999.

In terms of coping, we are most likely to do well when the demands are low, our ability is high and the consequences are not too significant. Unfortunately, many situations don't play out this way. The result is stress, anxiety and a reluctance to take a risk. In the case of promotion, this can lead us to change our minds and not apply for the job. So, changing the way we look at these three areas can positively influence our attitude. Ideally, we need to see the demands as not too high, our ability as being very high and the consequences as being manageable. Think about how you could apply this to a change situation that you are facing which requires you to be bold and take a risk. If you can reduce the demands, increase your confidence in your ability and have a more balanced perspective on the consequences then you are far more likely to cope with change.

Crooked thinking

Of course, changing our thinking is not always straightforward. Often it is made more difficult as we tend to entertain thoughts that seriously hamper our ability to think straight. Dr Albert Ellis, a world-famous psychologist, calls this *crooked thinking*. We are all guilty of engaging in it at certain times. Dr Ellis maintains that when we do so, it acts as a barrier to proper and effective thinking and good decision-making. Ferguson managed 212 players in the Manchester United first eleven during his 27-year reign. 'I've experienced most types of mindset,' he once noted. The following are the five most common different types of crooked thinking. Review them and identify which ones you are more inclined towards.

1 'Not fair' thinking

'David Beckham had a great talent for blocking out bad performances,' Ferguson says of the former England captain. 'I would give him stick and he would go off in a huff, probably thinking, "That manager's off his head, I was good today."' Beckham's inability to accept criticism was central to one of the most famous disputes in football.

Following a 2–0 defeat in an FA Cup tie at Old Trafford, Ferguson argued with Beckham about his lack of defensive effort in tracking back for Arsenal's second goal. Beckham refused to accept any criticism. 'He was around twelve feet from me,' Ferguson recalls. 'David swore at me and as I moved towards him, I kicked a boot which hit him right above the eye.' As he rose to retaliate, Beckham was restrained by his team-mates. 'Sit down. You've let your team down, you can argue as much as you like,' is what Ferguson said to his midfielder. 'When I called him in the next day to go through the video analysis, he still would not accept his mistake. It was in those days that I knew David had to go.' Whenever you can feel yourself engaging in 'not fair' thinking and start to believe that the world is out to stop you, remember the 'ultimatum game', which is the most well-known experiment in behavioural economics.

The rules of the game are simple. Two people are paired up and given £10 to divide between them.

According to this rule one person (the proposer) decides, on his own, what the ratio of the split should be (for example, 50:50, 70:30). He then makes a take-it-or-leave-it offer to the other person (the responder). The responder can either accept the offer, in which case both players pocket their share of the cash, or reject it, in which case both players walk away empty-handed. Now, if both players are rational, the proposer will keep £9 for himself and offer the responder £1, and the responder will take it. After all, whatever the offer, the responder should accept, since if he accepts, he will get some money and if he declines, he will get none. A rational proposer will realise this and make a low offer.

In practice, though, this very rarely happens. Instead, low offers – anything below £2 – are routinely rejected. Think about what this actually means. People would rather have nothing than let the other person walk away with too much of the money. They will give up free money to punish what they perceive as greedy or selfish behaviour. The interesting thing is that the proposer anticipates this – presumably because they know that they would act the same way if they were in the responder's shoes. As a result, the proposers don't make many low offers in the first place. The most common offer in the ultimatum game is, in fact, £5.

What makes this test even more interesting is what happens when the rules are changed. In the original version of the game, only luck determines who gets to be the responder and the proposer. So people feel that the split should be fairly equal. But people's behaviour in the game changes quite dramatically when the rules are altered. For instance, when the researchers decide that the proposers should earn the position through performing better in an exam, proposers offer significantly less money, which rarely gets rejected. If people think that a proposer merits his position, they feel he deserves to keep more of the money. What this test demonstrates is that most people want a reasonable relationship between what we achieve and what we deserve. In short, we are naturally inclined to play fair. Using 'not fair' thinking cannot be accepted as a justified response to things going wrong. Instead, look at your own efforts at dealing with change and decide whether you have done enough to deserve success.

2 Driver thinking

This is the kind of thinking where you believe that if you are unsuccessful something dire will happen. This can blind us to more important matters, and it was this type of thinking which was central to Ferguson's dispute with his talismanic captain, Roy Keane.

After one particularly poor defeat to Middlesbrough in 2005, the players found the injured Keane waiting for them in the dressing room after their first day back in training. His mood had not been helped when he heard that one of the poorest performers in the game, the young winger Kieran Richardson, had recently ordered himself a Bentley car. Keane loathed the concept of young players, who were just starting their careers, being lavished with the trappings of success. Richardson – who had announced to the dressing room on his return from the close season that from then on he should be addressed as Rico – was to Keane's thinking the epitome of everything that was going wrong, and Keane's verbal ambush was unrestrained.

If the players thought the storm had abated after this private ear-bashing, they were wrong. Keane was the studio guest on MUTV's show *Play the Pundit*, in which a player analyses a performance for the watching public, when it covered that defeat. 'There are no characters in this team any more,' Keane thundered. 'The players have been asked questions and they are just not coming up with the answers. I'm sick of having to say it and they are sick of listening.' Ferguson insisted that the show should not be aired, except in the United dressing room. When he viewed it, he accused Keane of ranting, of no longer thinking like the leader of Manchester United, of losing the key to the dressing room door.

'That intolerant streak in Roy was his undoing,' says Gary Neville. 'A few of the younger players in the team were in awe of Roy and I don't think they knew how to handle him. They tiptoed around him. You could see why they were intimidated by this hard man. The younger players needed to be allowed to come out of their shells but it was hard to see what would bring change about – until that infamous programme.' Days later, Ferguson terminated his contract and Keane left the club for good.

Steve Jobs started his billion-dollar Apple business in his garage when he was in his early twenties. He went on to lead the field in three separate industries, including music (where his iPod and iTunes have revolutionised the way music is delivered), movies (where Pixar is the most successful animation studio) and computing (where Apple's design is legendary). He was obviously an extraordinarily driven individual. What I liked about him is how he used his driver philosophy to inspire rather than inhibit. Whenever he was faced with a big decision, he asked himself the unforgettable driver question: 'What would I do if this was the last night of my life?' Asking this very same question helped him to meet his wife. He was speaking at a university and his wife-to-be was in the audience. He approached her after the event and she gave him her number. He wanted to take her out that night but there was a business meeting he had to attend. On the way to his car, he asked himself his driver question and upon answering it, ran back to the lecture hall, found the woman and took her out. They were together for the rest of his life.

Do you have your own inspiring – rather than deflating – driver question?

3 Stopper thinking

Stopper thinking is what happens when we start selling ourselves short and start saying things like, 'I'm useless, I can't do it, I'll make a mistake.' This attitude leads us to play it safe. It was best embodied by Eric Cantona. In 1997, at the relatively young footballing age of thirty, he suddenly retired. His team-mates weren't as surprised by this as they might have been, as they sensed that his attitude had changed markedly, that the spark had gone out of his game.

Cantona agrees with that assessment: 'I didn't want to play any more. I'd lost the passion. I retired so young because I wanted to improve every time, to be a better player. For myself and the team. To win trophies. To have the feeling of improving. When I retired, I didn't feel that I could improve any more. And I lost the passion at the same time. The passion comes with the motivation of improving. If you lose the passion, you lose the motivation. Money was never an issue,' he insists.

A recent study of international ice skaters before a major competition demonstrated that those who spent considerable time attempting new moves and making numerous mistakes during training performed better in the actual competition than those who only repeated what they could already do well. The risk-takers stopped worrying about making mistakes and performed with greater freedom and confidence.

It reminds me of the story of James Dyson, who first had the idea of inventing the bag-less vacuum cleaner back in 1972, twenty years before he made it available to buy. He created no fewer than 5,127 prototypes until he finally had a success. He had the following poem pinned on his workshop door to remind him to avoid falling into the trap of stopper thinking:

Rules for being human

You will learn lessons.
There are no mistakes – only lessons.
A lesson is repeated until it is learned.
If you don't learn lessons, they get harder
(Pain is one way the universe gets your attention).
You'll know you've learned a lesson when your actions change.

Anon

4 Illogical thinking

Illogical thinking is often used when we are under great pressure. It involves pursuing an approach without gaining all the relevant data.

Many sports people have superstitions or rituals which they go through and Sir Alex Ferguson was no different. Before every European game he would wear an old United jersey and a red woolly 'three feathers' Wales rugby hat – which he pinched from Ryan Giggs – when overseeing training sessions. When speaking to the media about Giggs, Ferguson said: 'The only thing that let Ryan down is he enabled me to steal his Welsh hat. He will never get it back, it has worked for me, my lucky bonnet for Europe. I stole it and always wear it. I think Ryan is too intimidated by me to even think he is going to get it back!'

But Ferguson never took the superstition completely seriously, because he recognised the dangers of illogical thinking. The following exchange, though an urban legend, is often mistakenly retailed as factual, and you can see why: it neatly highlights this kind of thinking.

Navy: Please divert your course fifteen degrees to the north to avoid a collision.
Civilian: Recommend that you divert your course fifteen degrees to south to avoid a collision.
Navy: This is the captain of a US Navy ship. I say again, divert your course.
Civilian: No! I say again, divert your course.

Navy: This is the aircraft carrier *Enterprise*. We are a large warship of the US Navy. Divert your course now!

Civilian: This is a lighthouse. Your call.

5 Over-generalising thinking

'Between me and you, I don't think I have any real weaknesses,' were the words written by Peter Schmeichel in his autobiography. This view of himself was consistent with other people's impressions. The Danish journalist Niels Rasmussen remembers a young player with 'an enormous amount of comfort in himself' – or as his national team-mate John Jensen put it, 'He believed in himself so much it was unbelievable.' This transmitted itself into all areas of Schmeichel's life. His instinctive reaction whenever he conceded a goal, which was to berate his team-mates, became a hallmark of his time at United. But his self-belief also allowed him to master other, off-pitch activities. 'His ability to manoeuvre his hands up and down a piano is as incredible as anything he accomplished on a football pitch,' is how journalist Daniel Harris describes Schmeichel's piano skills.

In the opening months of the 1998–99 season, Schmeichel began to attract criticism for a number of key mistakes he had made. It was during those winter months that he chose to announce that he was to leave

United, claiming that his body was 'unable to cope with the strain of English football'.

'It is easy to believe that the arrogance which unpinned his talent found this criticism difficult. You have to wonder whether this was what really prompted him to leave,' argues Daniel Harris. This view is strengthened by the fact that Schmeichel changed his mind two years later and returned to England to play for Aston Villa and Manchester City in the English League he had cited as being too physically demanding. The last symptom of crooked thinking is over-generalising. When you start to tell yourself that you will not be affected by change it can be dangerous as you start to miss obvious signs of change.

Or, indeed, icebergs.

> *In all my experience, I have never been in any accident of any sort worth speaking about. I have seen but one vessel in distress in all my years at sea. I never saw a wreck and never have been wrecked nor was I in any predicament that threatened to end in disaster of any sort.*
>
> E.J. Smith, captain, RMS *Titanic*, 1907

It's important to be aware of times when you slip into this kind of crooked thinking, and do something to stop and change the thought into a logical alternative.

Ring the Changes

Change itself contains the germ of happiness.

Charles Darwin

Do you remember the scene in *Fawlty Towers* where Basil Fawlty suggests that his wife Sybil should participate in *Mastermind* and choose 'The bleeding obvious' as a specialist subject? If you have already begun to adopt ideas explored in earlier chapters, you should be starting to face change with Alex Ferguson levels of confidence and the following two ideas may seem 'bleeding obvious', but I want to offer them as a quick reminder.

Bleeding Obvious 1: Play to your strengths

In the movie *Return of the Jedi*, Luke Skywalker persuades Darth Vader to turn against the evil emperor, saving his own life and restoring peace and hope to the galaxy, by turning to him and saying, 'I know there's still good in you. There's good in you. I can sense it.' At the start of this book, I suggested that you may already be naturally doing many things well. Playing to your own strengths is a technique which can help you avoid straying over to the Dark Side. All you have to do is sense the good in yourself.

One of the first changes which Sir Terry Leahy implemented as chief executive of Tesco was to change the format of a simple question which had a dramatic effect. When managers visited a store, they stopped asking, 'What could be improved?' and instead asked, 'What is going so well?' Leahy believes that this one change helped to create a climate of co-operation and openness simply by concentrating on strengths first.

This was similar to the approach that Alex Ferguson took during the famous treble season in 1999. Andy Cole recalls, 'We used to watch videos of our upcoming opponents and I don't think it did us any good because they were invariably the best bits. We'd watch a team like Monaco and think, "Fuck me, they're absolutely brilliant."' The players approached Ferguson and suggested that they play to their own strengths and let their opponents worry about them. 'We stopped looking at our opponents in such detail and look what happened,' Cole adds as evidence.

It is logical to assume that if you want to focus on doing well during change, and you want to make confident decisions, then you will be far more successful if you utilise your strengths as a platform. As obvious as this sounds, it is amazing how often people lose sight of their strengths at the very time they need to be focusing on them the most.

What are you really good at? What skills and attributes have got you to where you are today? What can you really rely on to deliver when the heat is on? What are you great at when you are operating in the zone?

The answers to these questions should point you towards your strengths and help you make choices about your actions and behaviour. I believe that all leaders have a responsibility to encourage this kind of thinking and focus on what people can do rather than what they can't.

Consider how you can pay attention to your strengths and be aware of how they work for you. Wayne Bennett, a legendary Australian rugby league coach, also believes this. He suggests that we all have a special talent and he says to his players, 'Don't die with the music in you!' Avoid being too modest but instead use your awareness to develop your confidence. We all have talents but we sometimes lack basic awareness of what these actually are. Spend some time reflecting on what you consider your signature strengths to be. Your strengths represent the things you really excel at. Things that you know you can rely on in yourself. Attributes and talents that people readily recognise in you. Understanding this and considering how you can use them more effectively will contribute to the creation of your own winning environment.

Ferguson describes some of his own key characteristics in his Harvard interviews on what he considers to be the requirements of a great leader. 'I am a gambler – a risk taker – and you can see that in how we played in the late stages of matches,' he says. 'If we were down with fifteen minutes to go, I was ready to take more risks. I was perfectly happy to lose 3–1 if it meant we'd given ourselves a good chance to draw or win. So in those last fifteen minutes, we'd go for it. We'd put in an extra attacking player and worry less about defence.' This strength was reflected in the frequency with which his sides would score crucial late goals.

If you find this difficult, go to the chapter on feedback ('Change the Record' pages 93–110), then approach your colleagues, family and friends. Talk to them about what they see your strengths to be and how valuable they are. Ask them how you could utilise these strengths more. These conversations will raise your self-awareness and your capacity to focus on your strengths when facing change. Make a list of your signature strengths and write down next to each one how you could use it more effectively.

Bleeding Obvious 2: Enjoy the ride

Sir Alex Ferguson once credited the Italian tenor Andrea Bocelli as one of his chief inspirations. 'I remember going to see the great opera singer,' Ferguson explained. 'I had never been to a classical concert in my life. But I am watching this and thinking about the coordination and the teamwork, one starts and one stops, just fantastic.' One other important characteristic of

Bocelli's is his famous ability to relax before a performance. If you saw him a half-hour or so before one of his performances, you would find him mellowed out. He makes jokes, he smiles, he chats. In fact, you could easily mistake him for an audience member.

This was a feature that Ferguson would occasionally bring to his dressing room an hour before the start of a big game. As Gary Neville explained, 'Although it's mostly serious, sometimes he'll lighten the mood. We'd always look forward to playing Aston Villa just to hear him mangle Ugo Ehiogu's name. "Make sure you pick up Ehugu, Ehogy, whatever his name is."' Neville smiled at the memory: 'We'd always chuckle at that one. He never quite got it right.'

We're often led to believe that we should approach big events, such as pressure-packed meetings, with a mindset of gritted, focused intensity that we know as 'the game face'. In truth, that impulse is mistaken. Preparation is the right time for intensity and scowls; performance is the time for lightness and ease. Here's why: practice is an act of construction. It's the place to stretch, to make mistakes and fix them. It's the time to reach and repeat, over and over, until you've built the reliable skill. It's the place to experience and embrace the arduous frustration that's part of the building process.

Performance, on the other hand, is a very different situation. You are not trying to construct the skill. You are trying to employ it; to be alert, to react to an un-folding set of possibilities. In these kinds of situations, the most productive mindset tends to be a light, broad, attentive focus; one that stays in the moment, and con-trols the emotional ups and downs. As the great acting coach Constantin Stanislavski put it, 'The rehearsals are the work; the performance is the relaxation.'

Gérard Houllier believed that Ferguson's 'enjoyment and enthusiasm is apparent to all. That enthusiasm is infectious to his players.' Is this the case within your teams? When people are enjoying themselves it's so much easier to feel confident and relaxed. The absence of fear is such a great antidote to the debilitating effects of pressure. Working with others in an environment which values fun and enjoyment is conducive to people going the extra mile and staying committed even when the odds are against them.

There is plenty of medical evidence to support the view that laughter can positively influence our health. Laughter reduces our levels of cortisol (a stress hormone) and can also benefit the immune system by increasing the number and activity of cells which help the body to fight against viral attacks. So, making the effort to engage in activities that make you laugh or being around people and things that you find amusing should be part of your plan.

Enjoying the moment is something that comes more naturally to some than others. If you find it difficult to absorb yourself in the present and simply enjoy it for its own sake then you may need to engage in some self-coaching. When you sense yourself getting overwhelmed, remind yourself that coping with change should also be fun. Look for opportunities to make things enjoyable and keep a smile on your face whenever you can. Did you know that, on average, a child laughs about 400 times a day? In contrast, an adult will only laugh about fifteen times.

What happens to the other 385 laughs, though? Why is it that when we step into the grown-up world of work, a sense of humour becomes a rare commodity? Too often, we are preoccupied with our own worries, stresses and the pressures of our lives and so the importance of fun doesn't even merit a mention, yet the relationship between leadership and fun is critical. Research carried out at Colorado University suggests that playing is more than just about having fun. It is through playing that all animals, including humans, learn to take on and master life's challenges.

A useful way of thinking about this is to imagine if you could open up the top of your head and see how your brain works. You would see a brain of two halves; a left and a right side. Although both sides look identical and work together most of the time, they have quite different ways of seeing the world. The left-hand side of your brain is the serious and analytical part. The right-hand side, however, allows you to see the bigger picture and enjoy a good laugh. When you are relaxed and playful, you start to work the right side of your brain more and this increases the likelihood of you being more creative and original.

The following poem reminds me to do just that:

The Risk Poem

To laugh is to risk appearing a fool,
To cry is to risk appearing sentimental and soft,
To reach out for another is to risk involvement,
To show up and expose your feelings is to risk
Exposing your inherent self,
To place your idea, your dreams, your desires before
People is to risk their loss,
To love is to risk not being loved in return,
To show strength is to risk showing weakness,
To do is to risk failure.
The greatest hazard in life is to risk nothing,
The person who risks nothing gets nothing, has
Nothing, is nothing.
He may avoid suffering, pain, sorrow, but he does
Not live, he does not love,
He has sold, forfeited freedom, integrity,
He is a slave, chained by safety, locked away by fear.
Because, only a person who is willing to risk not
Knowing the result is FREE.

Anon

Circle of Change

If you have built castles in the air, your work need not be lost; that is where they should be. Now put the foundations under them.

Henry David Thoreau

I hope that you have found this book to be an interesting read and have enjoyed the stories, anecdotes and exercises. However, knowledge is like having money in the bank. It is valuable but it is not by itself useful. Only when the money is converted into something does it become useful. The good news is that, unlike money, knowledge actually appreciates when you spend it, creating new insights and more knowledge. Whatever you have taken from this book is the same. Without action, it is fairly pointless. It takes energy and courage to do something positive with this information.

It's important that you take some time to formalise your plan and identify exactly what you are going to do as a result of the ideas presented here. The diagram on page 206 has eight wheel sections, each representing one of the central chapters of this book. You might like to photocopy or draw a version of this diagram. Then, rating the centre, or hub, of the wheel as 0 (totally dissatisfied) and the outer edge as 10 (totally satisfied), rank your level of satisfaction with each idea about surviving change by putting a cross on the relevant spoke.

Next, draw a line to join the crosses.

How balanced does the perimeter of your wheel look?

Are there any areas which you would like to improve?

Remember Sir Alex Ferguson's assertion that 'The thing I have done well is to manage change,' how ready are you to face change?

Now it's time to formulate and finalise your plan. This will involve revisiting and re-reading each section of the book with a real focus on what you will use and start to put into action. There is no correct way to do this, but however you do it, I hope this book will be a useful tool to help you survive and thrive in changing times.

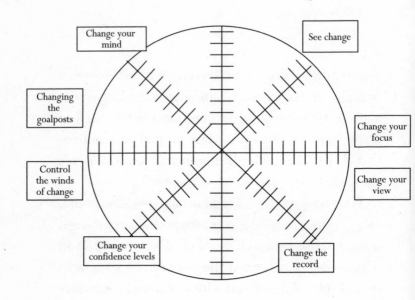

Change your mind

See change

Changing the goalposts

Change your focus

Control the winds of change

Change your view

Change your confidence levels

Change the record

A Final Thought

I started this book by remembering Sir Alex Ferguson's first day at Manchester United, so I think that it is appropriate to finish by recalling his words at his final home game as manager, when he told an emotion-drenched Old Trafford: 'Retirement doesn't mean it's the end. It's the start of a new chapter.'

Whatever position, status or ambitions you hold, change is all around us. To live means to accept change. Now we have reached the end of *How to Think Like Sir Alex Ferguson*, I sincerely hope you feel ready to start a new chapter and step out with a renewed confidence in your ability not to wither but to survive – and to thrive – in the face of change.

Start Where You Stand

Start where you stand and never mind the past,
The past won't help you in beginning new,
If you have left it all behind at last

Why, that's enough, you're done with it, you're through;
This is another chapter in the book,
This is another race that you have planned,
Don't give the vanished days a backward look,
Start where you stand.

The world won't care about your old defeats
If you can start anew and win success,
The future is your time, and time is fleet
And there is much of work and strain and stress;
Forget the buried woes and dead despairs,
Here is a brand new trial right at hand,
The future is for him who does and dares,
Start where you stand.

Old failures will not halt, old triumphs aid,
To-day's the thing, to-morrow soon will be;
Get in the fight and face it unafraid,
And leave the past to ancient history;
What has been, has been; yesterday is dead
And by it you are neither blessed nor banned,
Take courage, be brave and drive ahead,
Start where you stand.

Berton Braley

Good luck.

Acknowledgements

I would like to thank Geraldine, George and Rose for their continued inspiration, encouragement and support in letting me pursue my dreams. My parents, Brian and Rosemarie, for setting such an amazing example and offering inspiration on how to behave as a grown-up and my brothers, Anthony and Chris, and sister Rachael for their unfailing support and friendship. I would also like to extend my gratitude to Sir Alex Ferguson, the man whose example and professional courage made these anecdotes worth sharing.

This book is the end product of a great team. I'd like to thank the following people for their invaluable contribution. David Luxton offered the support of a great agent, Robin Harvie's enthusiasm and belief has been relentlessly positive and Blaise Tapp and Bernard Niven offered great research, insights and editing advice. Thank you also to the numerous people who generously gave insights, anecdotes and academic references but preferred to remain in the shadows. Finally, thanks to you, the reader, for your curiosity and for sharing your valuable time to read this book. I hope you enjoy it as much as I've enjoyed writing it.

Professor Damian Hughes
June 2014

Bibliography

Sir Alex Ferguson's management career:

Beckham, David. *My Side*, HarperSport, 2004.

Bruce, Steve. *Heading for Victory*, Bloomsbury, 1994.

Cantona, Eric. *My Story*, Headline, 1994.

Ferguson, Alex. *A Year in the Life*, Virgin Publishing, 1995.

— *A Will to Win*, Andre Deutsch Ltd, 1997.

— *Just Champion*, Manchester United Football Club, 1993.

— *Managing My Life*, Hodder & Stoughton, 2000.

— *My Autobiography*, Hodder & Stoughton, 2013.

— *Six Years at United*, Mainstream Publishing, 1992.

— *The Unique Treble: The Inside Story*, Hodder & Stoughton, 2000.

Giggs, Ryan. *My Life, My Story*, Headline, 2010.

Hughes, Mark. *Barca, Bayern and Back*, Hutchinson Radius, 1989.

Keane, Roy. *Keane*, Penguin Books, 2011.

McClair, Brian. *Odd Man Out*, Andre Deutsch Ltd, 1998.

McGrath, Paul. *Back From The Brink*, Random House, 2007.

Neville, Gary. *Red: My Autobiography*, Corgi, 2012.

Pallister, Gary. *Pally*, Know The Score, 2008.

Robson, Bryan. *Robbo: My Autobiography*, Hodder & Stoughton, 2012.

Rooney, Wayne. *My Decade In The Premier League*, HarperSport, 2013.

Schmeichel, Peter. *Schmeichel: The Autobiography*, Ted Smart, 1999.

Sharpe, Lee. *My Idea of Fun,* Orion, 2005.

Stam, Jaap. *Head To Head*, Collins Willow, 2001.

Other books on Manchester United and football:

Auclair, Philippe. *Cantona: The Rebel Who Would be King,* MacMillan, 2009.

Balague, Guillem. *Pep Guardiola,* Orion, 2013.

Calvin, Michael. *The Nowhere Men,* Arrow, 2014.

Carson, Mike. *The Manager,* Bloomsbury Paperbacks, 2014.

Charlton, Sir Bobby. *My Manchester United Years,* Headline, 2008.

Connley, Glenn. *How to Be Ferocious Like Sir Alex Ferguson,* Marshall Cavendish International Asia, 2011.

Crick, Michael. *The Boss,* Pocket Books, 2003.

Gillespie, Keith. *How Not to Be a Football Millionaire,* Trinity Mirror Sports Media, 2014.

Harris, Daniel. *The Promised Land,* Arena Sport, 2013.

Holt, Oliver. *If You Are Second, You Are Nothing,* Macmillan, 2006.

Hughes, Brian. *The King – Denis Law,* Empire Publications, 2004.

Kurt, Richard. *Red Devils,* Prion Books, 1998.

— *United! Dispatches from Old Trafford,* Mainstream Publishing, 1999.

— *United We Stood,* Sigma Leisure, 1994.

Kurt, Richard et al. *Deepest Red: An Anthology,* Portnoy Publishing, 2013.

Mitten, Andy. *Glory, Glory!,* Vision Sports Publishing, 2009.

— *We're the famous Man United,* Vision Sports Publishing, 2011.

Riley, Chris. *The Wit and Wisdom of Sir Alex Ferguson,* Biteback Publishing, 2013.

Strachan, Gordon. *My Life in Football,* Sphere, 2007.

Taylor, Daniel. *This is the One,* Aurum Press, 2007.

Torres, Diego. *The Special One,* HarperSport, 2014.

Vialli, Gianluca and Gabriele Marcotti. *The Italian Job,* Bantam Press, 2006.

Warnock, Neil. *The Gaffer,* Headline, 2014.

White, Jim. *Always in the Running,* Mainstream Publishing, 1996.

— *Are You Watching Liverpool?* William Heinemann Ltd, 1994.

— *Manchester United: The Biography,* Sphere, 2008.

Worrall, Frank. *Walking in a Fergie Wonderland,* John Blake Publishing, 2011.

Management, psychology and sport:

Abrahams, Dan. *Soccer Brain,* Bennion Kearny, 2013.

Bains, Gurnek et al. *Meaning Inc,* Profile Books, 2007.

Bannister, Dr Roger. *The First Four Minutes*, Sutton Publishing Ltd, 2004.

Bayliss, Dr Nick. *Wonderful Lives*, Cambridge Well Being Books, 2005.

Beilock, Sian. *Choke,* Constable, 2011.

Bennett, Wayne. *Don't Die With the Music in You,* ABC Books, 2002.

— *The Man in the Mirror,* ABC Books, 2008.

Beswick, Bill. *Focused for Soccer*, Human Kinetics Publishers, 2010.

Bolchover, David. *The Living Dead*, Capstone, 2005.

David and Chris Brady. *The 90 Minute Manager,* Prentice Hall, 2006.

Borg, James. *Persuasion*, Pearson, 2010.

Broadbent, Rick. *The Big If*, Macmillan, 2006.

Bronson, Po and Ashley Merryman. *Top Dog,* Ebury Press, 2013.

Brown, Derren. *Tricks of the Mind*, Channel 4 Books, 2006.

Bull, Steve. *The Game Plan*, Capstone, 2006.

Bull, Steve and Chris Shambrook. *Soccer: The Mind Game*, Reedswain, 2005.

Buzan, Tony. *Embracing Change*, BBC Active, 2006.

Cotterill, Stewart. *Team Psychology in Sports,* Routledge, 2012.

Dennis, Felix. *How To Get Rich*, Ebury Press, 2007.

Dourado, Phil. *The 60 Second Leader*, Capstone, 2007.

Ferguson, Penny. *Transform Your Life*, Infinite Ideas, 2006.

Fullan, Michael. *Leading in a culture of Change*, Jossey Bass, 2007.

Gibson, Clive, Mike Pratt, Kevin Roberts and Ed Weymes. *Peak Performance*, Profile Books, 2001.

Godin, Seth. *Meatball Sundae*, Piatkus, 2009.

Goldstein, Noah, Steve Martin and Robert Caldiani. *Yes!*, Profile Books, 2007.

Hamilton, Duncan. *Provided You Don't Kiss Me!*, Fourth Estate, 2007.

Helmstetter, Shad. *What to Say When You Talk to Yourself*, Grindle Pr Audio, 1986.

Katzenbach, Jon R. *Peak Performance*, Harvard Business School Press, 2000.

Lecky, Prescott. *Self-Consistency: A Theory of Personality,* Island Press, 1973.

Loehr, Jim. *The Only Way to Win,* Nicholas Brealey Publishing, 2012.

Mack, Gary. *Mind Gym*, McGraw Hill Professional, 2002.

Moorhouse, Adrian and Graham Jones. *Developing Mental Toughness*, Spring Hill, 2007.

Michels, Rinus. *Teambuilding*, Reedswain Publishing, 2013.

Nesti, Mark. *Psychology in Football, Routledge,* 2010.

Orlick, Terry. *In Pursuit of Excellence,* Human Kinetics Europe, 2007.

Peace, David. *The Damned United*, Faber and Faber, 2007.

Reeve, John Marshall. *Understanding Motivation and Emotion,* John Wiley and Sons, 2004.

Shinar, Yehuda. *Think Like a Winner*, Vermillion, 2007.

Stafford, Tom and Matt Webb. *Mind Hacks: Tips and Tools for Using Your Brain,* O'Reilly Media, 2004.

Steel, John. *Pitch Perfect*, John Wiley and Sons, 2006.

Sutton, Robert. *The No Asshole Rule*, Piatkus, 2010.

Taleb, Nassim Nicholas. *The Black Swan*, Penguin, 2008.

Taylor, David. *The Naked Coach*, Capstone, 2007.

Thompson, Jim. *The Double-Goal Coach,* William Morrow, 2003.

Turnbull, Professor Gordon. *Trauma,* Bantam Press, 2011.

Tutu, Desmond. *No Future Without Forgiveness*, Rider and Co., 1999.

Ungerleider, Steve. *Mental Training for Peak Performance*, Rodale Press, 2007.

Van Kaam, Adrian. *Existential Foundations of Psychology,* Doubleday, 1969.

Watson, James. *Avoiding Boring People*, OUP Oxford, 2007.

Williams, Jean. *Applied Sports Psychology: Personal Growth to Peak Performance,* Mayfield Publishing Co., 1998.

Williams, Steve. *Golf at the Top*, Amorata Press, 2005.

Wiseman, Richard. *Quirkology*, Macmillan, 2007.

Zander, Ben and Rosamund Stone Zander, *The Art of Possibility*, Harvard Business School Press, 2000.

Other sources:

British GQ
Daily Telegraph
Guardian
Harvard Business Review
Herald
Mail On Sunday, Gary Neville column
Manchester Evening News
New Statesman
Red Issue fanzine
Scotsman
United We Stand fanzine
Class Of '92 – 2013, Gabe And Benjamin Turner (DVD)
Sky Sports